After Development

After Development
The Transformation of the
Korean Presidency and Bureaucracy

SUNG DEUK HAHM
L. CHRISTOPHER PLEIN

GEORGETOWN UNIVERSITY PRESS / WASHINGTON, D.C.

Georgetown University Press, Washington, D.C. 20007
© 1997 by Georgetown University Press. All rights reserved.
Printed in the United States of America.
10 9 8 7 6 5 4 3 2 1   1997
THIS VOLUME IS PRINTED ON ACID-FREE OFFSET BOOKPAPER.

Library of Congress Cataloging-in-Publication Data

Hahm, Sung Deuk.
    After development : transformation of the Korean presidency and
  bureaucracy / Sung Deuk Hahm and L. Christopher Plein.
        p.   cm.
    Includes bibliographical references.
    1. Korea (South)—Politics and government—1960–1988. 2. Korea
  (South)—Politics and government—1988- . 3. Presidents—Korea
  (South). 4. Bureaucracy—Korea (South). 5. Technology and state—
  Korea (South). I. Plein, L. Christopher. II. Title.
  JQ1725.H345 1997
  352.23'095195—dc21
  ISBN 0-87840-639-5 (cloth)   ISBN 0-87840-660-3 (pbk.)
                                                      96-47406

Contents

Preface

This book explores the dynamic changes now under way in South Korea's political and institutional arrangements. In recent years, economic and political factors have converged to loosen the grip of authoritarian power over Korean economy and society. Indeed, Korea is on the threshold of becoming a "postdevelopmental" state where social and economic pressures will challenge existing institutional structures. In short, Korea's transition to more liberal and democratic institutional arrangements is not yet guaranteed. Through an analytical framework which seeks to take into account the influences of social and cultural factors as well as the incentives and motives of individual actors, a portrait of institutional transition is provided. These experiences are discussed against the backdrop of technology development and transfer, a policy area of critical importance to Korea's rapid modernization and economic development. This book finds that the role of bureaucracy is likely to change in the face of social transformation. We also find that the role of the president is undergoing substantial transformation. Where presidents once enjoyed absolute power over institutions, they must now increasingly act as brokers among often competing private interests and public actors.

The authors approach this subject from different backgrounds and perspectives. Sung Duek Hahm, who initiated this project, has interests in policy analysis, technology policy, comparative public policy, and institutional development and evolution in Korea, especially as it relates to the Korean presidency. He brings to the effort a deep grounding in Korean politics and administration. Christopher Plein became involved in this project through his interest in technology issues and policy, comparative policy and administration, and political institutions. His interest in the project stems particularly from the ramifications of globalization in economic and political arrangements.

This book is the product of a multiyear collaborative effort by both authors. Indeed, the purpose of writing this book was to bring together strands of research that we have been working together on for some time. Much of the research and analysis presented in this book first saw the light of day as conference papers. Some of the findings and observations have been published. For example, chapter 4 draws heavily from a piece of ours published in *Comparative Politics*, while chapter 5 is an outgrowth and extension of research we published in *Policy Studies Journal*. Over the past year, we refined our arguments and further developed our evidence that illustrate the profound transitions now under way in South Korea. While all-in-all this has been a collaborative effort, the burden of effort was shared in different ways. In particular, Sung Deuk Hahm undertook efforts to obtain and analyze the data on technology transfer and foreign direct investments, while both authors worked closely together to develop the book's analytical framework and findings.

This book has benefited from the generosity of others. Sung Deuk Hahm would like to thank Colin Campbell, Director of the Georgetown University Public Policy Institute; Alan Andreasen, Associate Dean of the Georgetown School of Business; David Walker, Director of the Center for Business-Government Relations of the Georgetown University School of Business; Wanki Paik, Dean of Korea University School of Politics and Economics; Moonsuk Ahn, Dean of Korea University Graduate School of Policy Studies; and Jaeho Yeom, Chair of the Department of Public Administration at Korea University, who helped Sung Deuk Hahm in arranging a teaching schedule that was amenable to writing this book. Sung Deuk Hahm is also grateful for grants from Georgetown University Graduate School, Georgetown University School of Business, Korean Institute for Legislative Studies, and International Leadership Academy. In addition, Stanford University's Hoover Institution provided facilities for Sung Deuk Hahm during the summer of 1996.

Finally, Sung Deuk Hahm would like to express his appreciation for the love and support that his mother and his wife, Jungmi Oh, have both shown throughout the writing of this book. He is also grateful for his daughters, Gari and Jini, who have inspired him to the best he can be.

Christopher Plein would like to acknowledge the positive climate of research and inquiry provided by his colleagues at West Virginia University and to express his appreciation for the support that his wife Stewart has shown through this and other projects.

Both authors deeply appreciate the role that John Samples, director of Georgetown University Press, played in the development of this book. His insights, support, and criticism were all crucial to realizing this effort. We also owe a debt of gratitude to the editorial staff at Georgetown University Press, especially Patricia Rayner, who have helped in the book's production. We also thank several reviewers whose comments led directly to improvements in this manuscript. Similarly, we would like to express our appreciation for the helpful comments, feedback, and suggestions that have been made by others over the past several years for the research that we have pursued on postdevelopmental transformation, institutional arrangements, and technology policy matters in Korea.

After Development

1

Introduction

INTRODUCTION

The course of inquiry is shaped in large part by changes in our social and political context. Extensive change in political systems throughout the world is providing an impetus for study and analysis. Over the past decade, numerous states have undergone regime changes. The breakup of the Soviet Union and various Eastern European states has created new countries, which have been fabricated from deep cultural roots but have underdeveloped economies and uncertain institutional arrangements. In Latin America, the rough edges of authoritarianism have been smoothed in many countries by pressures brought by domestic and international sources. In East Asia, the powerful economies of Korea and Taiwan have helped to pave the way for transitions from strict authoritarian regimes to the development of nascent democratic institutions and tolerance of social liberalization. The decline of authoritarian states in Eastern Europe and elsewhere has prompted a spate of research efforts on regime change and dynamics which is reminiscent in scope and ambition to studies carried out on modernization and development some forty years ago. A number of authors have sought to capture the nature and possible causes of these transitions (see, for example, Casper and Taylor 1996; Gasiorowski 1995; Haggard and Kaufman 1995). Against this backdrop of sociopolitical change and increasing scholarly inquiry, we can begin to consider the experiences of specific states undergoing transition from rigid authoritarian arrangements to the more open and liberal market and social arrangements that we associate with democratization.

The developmental experiences of authoritarian states have long been of interest to scholars. One of the reasons for this is that in some highly visible cases, such as Korea and Taiwan, experiences have contradicted models of development and modernization embraced by many in the scholarly and policy community. For example, in the case of Korea, authoritarian power intensified as economic development progressed through the 1970s and early 1980s.[1] As these authoritarian regimes have lost influence and undergone transformation since the late 1980s, there is renewed interest in the authoritarian experience in developmental states. Our interest rests squarely here, and indeed this book seeks to offer some insights on the causes and dimensions of authoritarian transformation in Korea. But our interests are also prospective, for our observations suggest that Korea is now on the threshold of what might be termed a "postdevelopmental" era.

Simply put, the postdevelopmental state is the product of turmoil created by profound social and economic upheaval which renders the role of established government institutions uncertain. Thus, as we will detail throughout the book, the twin forces of mass demands for social liberalization and demands by private interests to be unfettered from state market intervention have provided the momentum for this transformation. We also argue that matters of technology and their associated policy dimensions provide a good illustration of the complexities and challenges shaping the postdevelopmental state. In short, the postdevelopmental environment is characterized by a number of factors. For example, one distinguishing trait is domestic instability brought about by cross-cutting social concerns. These might be manifested in consumer demands for lower inflation rates and greater product availability, in labor demands for higher wages, and in enfranchisement for groups previously at a disadvantage. We might also expect policy contests to take on a zero-sum dimension because of perceptions of fixed resources and limited government abilities to influence future events. Such contests have a tendency to break down broad coalitions and factionalize sectoral and other interests. In such an environment, the broad categories of capital and labor dissolve. Another trait can be characterized as postmaterial concerns that concentrate on intractable policy issues, such as environmental quality, technological risk, and other public welfare issues. Inglehart (1977) identified such concerns as characteristic of postindustrial Western societies. In addition, recent research suggests that we may well expect these concerns to be manifested in newly industrialized states (see Abramson and Inglehart 1995; Lee 1994).

The societal dynamics of the postdevelopmental state are reflected in government institutions. This is well-illustrated in the case of Korea, where the decline of strong presidential arrangements is giving way to new and uncertain institutional arrangements. The courts, legislature, local governments, and, indeed, the bureaucracy will all benefit from the shift of power away from a strong executive. But the empowerment of these institutions will not necessarily translate into enhanced influence and efficacy on the part of the state vis-a-vis society. It goes without saying that the ideal of shared power brings with it the conflicts, contradictions, and compromises that we associate with decentralized governmental arrangements. And in terms of influence over matters of social and especially economic activity, the institutions of the postdevelopmental state have diminished abilities. Indeed, this is the key trait of the postdevelopmental state where the priorities and abilities of private capital are outstripping the capacity of the state to control the marketplace and the path of economic development.

To present our perspective on institutional transition, we seek to chart the historical changes in the Korean authoritarian state, to offer explanations for behavior taken by executive and bureaucratic actors, and to outline potential developments through an analysis that makes use of three analytical devices. First, in contrast to the developmental state literature, we focus on the Korean presidency as a benchmark for studying changes in the Korean developmental state. The developmental state literature tends to distinguish and concentrate on three primary players in the political arena: the state, capital (capitalists), and labor. The dynamics of development tend to be centered on the evolutions and tensions among these players. The literature on Korea is no exception to these broad distinctions (for a discussion, see D. Kang 1995). However, such distinctions, at least when referring to the state, are too crude. The state, as it were, is not a monolith, but is made up of many different actors. This simple observation is all too often overlooked, and as a result some misperceptions have been manifested about the nature of the Korean governmental apparatus.

Foremost among these has been the assumption of a powerful bureaucracy. This misconception is a reflection of a lumping together of the presidency and administrative apparatus into one monolithic whole. In Korea, this has been far from the case. As detailed later, broad policy strategies and formulation have traditionally been the domain of a strong president who has relied on an inner circle of advisors in the executive office (i.e., the Blue House). Absent other strong institutions, such as a legislature, courts, or a viable political party system to articulate counterproposals or to serve as a check on executive power, the bureaucracy has been the primary actor serving as a counterpoint to the president. Confusing the two as unified has served to underestimate the power of the president and overestimate the power of the bureaucracy (see Amsden 1989; Evans 1995; Fields 1995; Haggard 1990; Johnson 1987; Woo 1991). However, as it is the primary player in dictating policy through Korea's developmental experience, there is a clear case for focusing on the presidency.[2] In our study of the executive, we are particularly interested in presidential–bureaucratic relations and how they have changed over time.

To do this, our second analytical device is an interpretative framework which combines elements of structural determinism and rational choice theory. Through such an approach, we can capture the effects of both cultural and social conditions and changing social and political events on the activities of individual policy actors. Furthermore, building on the first analytical device, by decoupling the president and his inner circle from the strong and determined role of the state, we can note the internal tensions that make up the dynamics of the executive–bureaucratic relationship.

To give some order to what might otherwise be an expansive treatment of the authoritarian state, our third device is to limit our analysis to events and circumstances surrounding the evolution of technology policy in Korea. Technological requirements and technology market forces may outstrip the capacity of the strong state to determine economic activity (Wade 1992), as is the emerging trend in the Korean case. As a key component to general development strategies aimed at expanding Korea's economic and industrial capacities, policies related to technology transfer, acquisition, and development have played a crucial role. Therefore, we examine the nature and the limits of state policy intervention by the Korean presidency and bureaucracy and their influence on technology policy and technology-transfer strategies.

In short, this book explores the emergence of the postdevelopmental state in Korea by focusing on the transformational role of the presidency and bureaucracy in charting the country's development objectives, policy strategies, and tactics. This book focuses primarily on the changing role of the presidency and the bureaucracy in influencing state industrial and technological development.

THE PLAN OF THE BOOK

This book is divided into three parts. In chapter 2, we introduce the motives and purposes of our study. In chapter 3, we outline the structural–rational framework which undergirds our emphasis on studying the effects of history and change on policy actors and their actions. Next, in the second part of the book, we turn our attention to the presidential role in technology policy by investigating technology-policy arrangements in general and then concentrating on technology-transfer policies utilized by Korea since the early 1960s. Finally, we turn our attention to a discussion of the prospects of institutional evolution in the postdevelopmental state.

We now briefly review the content of each chapter, so that the reader may have a sense of how the book unfolds.

Chapter 2 introduces the motives and purposes of our study by providing a brief overview of authoritarian transition in Korea. In this chapter we emphasize the need to disassemble the constituent parts that make up the state in order to understand better the institutional forces at work in regime transition. We also give emphasis to the developmental and postdevelopmental state experience to point out how structural conditions are shaping institutional arrangements. We set this discussion against a backdrop of past literature.

Chapter 3 concentrates on the presentation and initial application of the theoretical framework that is at the foundation of this analysis. Specifically, this chapter first provides a discussion of the structural–rational framework for bureaucratic behavior. In this chapter we explain how structural forces, such as history and socioeconomic environment, create constraints and context for actions of individual governmental actors to be carried out. To develop the framework, we need to discuss both the structural and the rational-choice perspectives, citing literature and putting it in perspective for our purposes. In presenting the framework, we describe the structural and rational foundations of the evolution of modern Korean executive–bureaucratic politics.

Using a structural–rational framework, we investigate the apparent decline of authoritarian arrangements within Korea. Not surprisingly, a structuralist perspective illustrates how changing socioeconomic conditions, especially in terms of the growth of absolute influence of capital interests and the emergence of popular democratic movements, have helped precipitate the decline of the authoritarian state. Most interestingly, a rational-choice perspective allows us to see how political leaders unwittingly accelerated the decline of authoritarian arrangements. By pursuing short-term strategies, these elites helped to put into place the conditions necessary for long-term social and economic liberalization.

Chapter 4 explores the dynamic relationship between presidential elites and bureaucrats in matters relating to technology policy. A structural perspective allows us to see how the transformation of the Korean economy and larger international forces have placed a premium on technology-oriented policy. These changing conditions have resulted in new administrative arrangements and executive–bureaucratic relationships due to a premium on technical expertise in the policy formulation and implementation process. A rational-choice perspective allows us to see how the changing dynamic of technology policy has altered conditions of influence and prestige in the bureaucracy.

Chapter 5 explores the dynamics of policy control over flows of foreign investment into Korea through regulation of foreign direct investment and technology licensing. The primary finding of this chapter is that the Korean government has had much greater discretion and influence over the flow and content of foreign investment and presence in the economy than is usually ascribed to the developmental state. In this chapter we focus closely on the interaction of bureaucratic and executive relations, objectives, and interactions. A structural perspective helps to illustrate how international and domestic factors have constrained the extent of discretion over the course of foreign investment regulation. A rational-choice perspective helps to explain the motives of individual policy-maker activities, especially as seen in context of presidential–bureaucratic arrangements relating to technology transfer.

Most illustrative of this are actions taken by the Chun regime aimed at shoring up support among capital interests. These actions contradicted the path of development that would have been expected under a purely structuralist framework. In sum, domestic factors, such as the need for a transition from agrarian to industrial sources and a large supply of labor, helped to shape the policy actions of the early part of Korean modernization. International forces, such as the move to high-technology production processes, have recently altered policy choices. The experience helps to illustrate both the extent and the limits of policy control over technology-transfer patterns.

Chapter 6 closes the book by summing up the experiences of Korea in the context of larger questions surrounding the prospects of institutional transformation in the postdevelopmental state. In this chapter, we give particular focus to changes facing the Korean presidency. We revisit our theses on how the twin forces of democratization and economic liberalization are shaping institutional arrangements in Korea. In doing so, we review the major contours or elements of the developmental state in transition. We then turn our attention to what the future might hold for a postdevelopmental Korea. In making these observations, we invite the reader to consider how similar circumstance might arise in other newly industrialized states.

A PREVIEW OF OUR FINDINGS

In the past decade, Korea has undergone profound political change. The transformation of Korean politics and institutional arrangements has been overshadowed on the global stage by sweeping transformations in Eastern Europe and the former Soviet Union. But the transformation of a capitalistic authoritarian regime provides the opportunity to develop explanations and draw lessons, just as the demises of command economies do. As we argue in this book, this transformation is best understood by evaluating how the structural effects of historic factors, contemporary domestic events, and international pressures have affected the behavior of Korean presidents and bureaucracy. As we will show, such an approach is best executed through the use of an interpretive framework that combines elements of structural determinism with rational-choice models. Applied to the key policy area of technology transfer and development, our analysis yields a number of findings and observations relating to the Korean experience specifically and to development state transition in general.

One of our most important observations deals with the emergence of the postdevelopmental state as a product of both structural conditions and the individual actions of key political players. Various conditions have contributed to the rise of the postdevelopmental state. Success in economic planning by authoritarian regimes conveyed legitimacy to the state until a critical threshold was reached at which social and economic expectations overwhelmed state capacity. In the postdevelopmental state, both social and economic actors often view the state more as part of the problem than as a means of addressing concerns, demands, and needs. In such arrangements, the state is no longer seen as the key player in determining the course of economic development and societal arrangements. Coupled with the institutional decentralization that has followed the decline of authoritarian arrangements, such a diminished status for the state changes the structure of incentives, awards, and consequences for individual behavior within the altered institutional environment. In short, there are more opportunities for action, greater uncertainties for success with the multiple veto points developed in arrangements where power is shared by many policy actors, and less risk involved in losing in conflicts and contests due to the decline of personality-driven authoritarian arrangements.

Our interest in how the state has lost ground in the face of the growing autonomy of capital interests is the second major theme of this work. The declining influence of the state over economic and, by extension, social matters is a hallmark of what we call the postdevelopmental experience. As we will note, structural factors have contributed to these conditions. But we also seek to emphasize how short-term actions by policy actors are also responsible for these developments. The rational-choice perspective is particularly useful here. Because individual policy action has been as central to developmental state transformation as structural conditions, we describe how the short-term time horizons of policy actors may lead to undesirable long-term consequences for these actors. The transformation of the Korean state to a more decentralized and democratic arrangement is in large part the unintended consequence of actions taken by the authoritarian regime of President Chun Doo Hwan. Chun made concessions to capital interests in a short-term effort to shore up political support in the face of rising popular dissent from students, labor, and the middle class. This is a clear example of how short-term rational expectations can lead to long-term consequences that work against the initiator of policy action. The result of concessions made by the Chun regime served to strengthen the hand of capital interests by giving them greater financial autonomy. Freed from restrictions imposed by the state, capital interests, largely in the form of business conglomerates known as *chaebols*, have been able to pursue product and manufacturing strategies independent of the state. This has served to hasten the demise of the authoritarian state and has left an uncertain legacy for future governments.

Our third major observation deals with institutional transformation in the postdevelopmental state. We argue that the Korean presidency will remain the prevailing influence in the policy-making process for the foreseeable future. However, the power of the institution will be far from absolute. Instead, institutional transformation will focus more on the ability of the president to act as a broker and facilitator in the policy process. Instead of imposition of will, presidential success will be predicated on the ability to resolve conflict among various interests and to build the coalitions necessary to achieve policy objectives. We also observe that the president will become more dependent upon the bureaucracy due to the complexities involved in dealing with contemporary policy issues. In such circumstances, the influence of the bureaucracy will be strengthened in terms of influencing policy formulation and implementation. We suggest that the presidency will become less personality-driven and more institutional in nature. In short, technical, economic, and social forces have combined to erode the absolute power of the president over policy direction. Korean presidents are now more receptive to technological policy concerns and enlisting the advice of those outside the president's inner circle. Such a shift signals an important change in the nature of the Korean presidency and its interaction with the bureaucracy; by extension, this becomes a key dimension in understanding the dynamics of developmental transition in Korea.

CONCLUSION

The prevalence of regime change and transitions in the world community invite inquiry and discussion as to the causes and consequences of such transformations. We seek to contribute to such explorations through an investigation of developmental state transition in Korea. We will concentrate on two dimensions of this multifaceted topic. One dimension is institutional, involving as it does the evolution and role of the presidency and bureaucracy in the Korean state. The other dimension is policy-oriented, and here we concentrate our attention on matters relating to technology transfer and development. We believe that both reflect well on, and are critical to, the transformation of the Korean state and society. In the chapters that follow, we further develop the analytical framework by which we interpret these dimensions and further explore dimensions relating to technology policy. We now must turn to a fuller discussion of how the developmental state has been characterized in the literature and what traits have come to reflect the postdevelopmental state. These and other matters are the focus of our next chapter.

NOTES

1. In this book we refer to the Republic of Korea, or South Korea, as Korea.

2. The power of the president and the tensions between the president and administrative nexus are evident in controversies that emerged in the 1970s between President Park Chung Hee and the Economic Planning Board (EPB). Against the advice of EPB and other administrative actors, President Park and his inner circle decided to forge ahead with a heavy industrialization program. This plan was ill-conceived and exposed Korea to downturns in the world market caused by oil shocks and runaway inflation. Korean industry was overextended and growth slowed. The motives of President Park's actions seemed to have been primarily political, so as to forge a coalition of support among a few powerful *chaebols* and to develop a defense capability in an uncertain world where the U.S. military assistance might decline (E. Kim 1994).

2

Korea in Transition

THE KEYS TO SUCCESS: A LEGACY OF DIFFERING THEORETICAL INTERPRETATIONS

A small and overpopulated country, Korea is poorly endowed with natural resources. However, one well-recognized attribute has been its relatively skilled and devoted workforce. Despite extraordinary constraints, many challenges have been surmounted to achieve economic development objectives. For example, to meet the problem of a small domestic market, Korea pursued international export markets; to solve the lack of product technology, they borrowed foreign technologies; and to compensate for the problem of natural resource shortages, they imported with the foreign exchange they earned from industrial exports (Collins 1990; Krueger 1990; Westphal 1990). Since the early 1960s, Korea has been transformed from a predominantly agricultural economy to a newly industrialized one (see Choi 1986 for a detailed discussion of industrial transformation). Today Korea stands on the verge of postindustrial status, as services and high-technology activities make up an increasing part of the economic base.

Over the past decade, considerable research has been dedicated to how and how well the strong authoritarian state controls and promotes economic and industrial growth in Korea. However, the literature has generally underappreciated the role of the distinct institutions which make up the Korean state. Instead the state has been treated as a monolithic entity; debate and discussion of the appropriate role of the state in economy have followed the familiar distinction between neoclassical and developmental state approaches. Because of this, institutional arrangements within Korea, such as a strong presidency and its bureaucratic nexus, have not been given their due in inquiry and analysis. This

11

literature, developed and reaching its maturity during an era of industrial (economic growth-oriented) policy schemes, has also underestimated the substantive distinctions brought by newly emergent postindustrial or postmaterial policy concerns associated with political democratization and economic internationalization.

From the neoclassical perspective, relatively unrestricted market forces are the key to effective macroeconomic performance. Economic development success is achieved through public policies that effectively orient the domestic economy to international market arrangements (see Balassa, 1981; 1982; Krueger 1979, 1995; Ranis and Fei 1975; Westphal 1978). Those who ascribe to the neoclassical position do not, for the most part, claim that free markets guarantee total societal and economic success. Rather, the underlying assumption of this position is that market imperfections are more desirable than public policy imperfections that interfere with economic activity (see Colclough, 1991:7). This leads to a bias against considering the role of the state in guiding market activities that will achieve the economic development objectives that are often held up as benchmarks of market success. Thus, such assumptions tend to underplay, and often criticize, the role that political institutions play in achieving these goals. As a result, the highly active role that Korean institutional actors have played in comprehensive economic and industrial planning and the implementation of measures that made it possible for Korea to control technological inflows and deepen its technological capacities have sometimes been overlooked (see Chang 1993; Clark and Chan 1994; Jones and Sakong 1980; Johnson 1987; Mardon 1990; Wade 1992). Indeed, the evidence on Korea runs counter to neoclassical assumptions and positions on economic development.

The developmental state approach ascribes Korea's successful industrialization process to strong and competent *bureaucratic* dominance over the parochial interests of private actors. This view stipulates a deliberate targeting of selected industries for development, through a strategy that (1) concentrates on the sector's development for a preplanned period; (2) assimilates foreign technologies to assist development; (3) applies the experience gained to the next phase of the economic development; and (4) proceeds to increasingly sophisticated industries and technologies (see Amsden 1989; Deyo 1987; Haggard and Moon 1990; Johnson 1982; Wade 1990). By drawing attention to the political and administrative aspects of economic development, the developmental state approach has made an important contribution (see Moon and Prasad 1994).

However, the developmental state approach does not fully capture the dynamics of state influence and strength which varies across time and issues (see Cheng 1990; Donor 1992; E-Y Kim 1993). In the case of Korea, the developmental state approach has neglected the highly active role of the presidency in comprehensive industrial development planning. The developmental state approach has all too often concentrated on the strong state as a unitary actor or, at best, has been biased toward bureaucratic actors. In the Korean case, such a perspective undervalues the dominance that the presidency has historically had over bureaucratic actors and how personal preferences have often overruled bureaucratic policy recommendations. The influence of the president becomes particularly evident when seen in the context of technological development as a device for economic and industrial development. Here, too, the developmental state approach has underappreciated the importance of technology as a factor in development. In other words, as we noted earlier, what the developmental state approach (see Amsden 1989; Fallows 1994) underestimates is that technological requirements and technological market facets may outstrip the capacity of the state to determine economic activity (Wade 1992). This is the emerging trend with Korea.

In the case of Korea, a limited literature has emerged on the dynamics of state intervention into the economy through industrial and technology-development policy. Cheng (1990) provides an overview of the role that regime dynamics have played in Korean industrial development policy schemes. For instance, Cheng (1990:139) argues that, "A careful specification of regime dynamics—the gaining or losing of political legitimacy, the weakening or reconsolidation of political power—is necessary to assess how political variables impinge on development processes [in Korea]." His work provides a linkage between the abstract goals of technology-based industrial development and the need to reward and cultivate political support. Kim and Dahlman (1992) discuss the role that technology-oriented policies have played in the

Korean development experience. Their perspective, which out-
lines how both supply and demand are needed for technological
innovation and adoption, emphasizes the role that government
plays as a linkage between these two dimensions. They argue that
early in Korea's development the government sought to provide
linkages for technological supply and demand situations that did
not yet exist. But they offer a sanguine view of Korea's policy initiatives, holding that they have ultimately been successful.

With the current pattern of social democratization and technological development, Korea has begun to reflect generalizations
made by several scholars that the modern state is now the agent
of a coalition of interests, which may vary from issue to issue, but
is rooted in shared perceptions of long-term interests (Okimoto
1989). Hall (1986:17) provides an apt description, noting that
"The state appears as a network of institutions, deeply embedded
within a constellation of ancillary institutions associated with
society and the economic system. Contemporary states do not
seem to be as autonomous from societal influence as state-centric
theories imply." More specifically, others argue that state industrial polices have been to a great extent subjected to the political
calculus of legitimacy-building, power consolidation, and regime
survival (Haggard 1990; Haggard and Moon 1990; Moon and
Prasad 1994). In order to ensure regime survival, political leadership is forced to consolidate power (Y. Kim 1994). The process of
consolidating power involves building a coalition, which induces
political leadership to align and realign itself with diverse social
forces through cooptation, appeasement, containment, or even
punishment. In this regard, state industrial policies are strategic
instruments of political leadership used to maintain power and to
cultivate and refine bases of support. These coalitional dynamics
and policy choices make relations between the state and social
forces dynamic, precarious, and uncertain. In this climate, this
implies that the state must confer extensively with other societal
actors prior to effecting a change in industrial policies (Schmidt
1996). Implementation of new and revised policies also depends
on the cooperation of these actors. As a result, the role of government policy is complex and often subject to cross-cutting pressures. In such conditions, the ability of government to encourage
and practice policy coordination becomes both paramount and
challenging.

THE DYNAMICS OF AUTHORITARIAN TRANSITION

Since the early 1960s, Korea has been dominated by strong presidents seeking to exert control over all aspects of the policy process. Other institutions, such as the legislature, political parties, and interest groups, were noticeably underdeveloped and played a subordinate role in the policy process. Only the bureaucracy, often working in concert with business interests, evolved to temper the absolute control of the president. The absolute influence of the president was very noticeable in matters relating to industrial and technological development. But this picture of a president-centered state is beginning to change.

The twin forces of social liberalization, which most prominently has taken the form of democratization, and economic reform, which is driven in large part by the changing nature of technology, are leading to a greater emphasis on institutionalization and a move away from personality-driven policy arrangements. This movement is a result of demands that government be more responsive to sectoral and public demands and better skilled at handling the complexities of technology-related issues. The result is a movement away from a system in which authority over policy is imposed by the president and his closest advisors. In its place, a system is emerging in which the president still plays a major role in policy guidance and direction, but emphasis is increasingly placed on his ability to arrive at courses of policy action as a *broker* among divergent and often competing bureaucratic and sectoral interests.

Democratization is changing the face of Korean society and politics. The return of a civilian president and the emergence of nascent opposition parties are but the most visible signs of this sea change. Other developments include a legislature which is more emboldened to comment on policy areas that were once the president's sole domain and the emergence of a public voice that is amplified through the press and organized interests. In the social dimension, democratization coupled with the emergence of a consumer-oriented society has brought domestic instability. This is reflected in rising incomes and changing attitudes toward manual jobs and the traditional work ethic. These demographic changes and the rise of labor movements have contributed to an increase in wage rates in recent years. As a consequence, Korea now faces increasing competition in international markets for labor-intensive, low- and medium-technology goods (for discussion, see E. Kim 1994). Both these domestic and international factors create pressures to reconsider development strategies, especially toward technological innovation.

Under these circumstances, the complexity of policy planning for technological innovation has vested greater influence in the hands of those in the bureaucracy with jurisdiction over matters relating to science and technology. Those within the higher circles of the office of the president are wrestling with the fact that economic planning will require the input of these bureaucratic echelons' interests. As we will detail later, overcoming past practices which saw the president imposing his will over the bureaucracy may meet some difficulty. Compounding the ascendancy of administrative actors are the forces of political and economic liberalization. Political change has taken the form of democratization. This has been most clearly expressed in terms of an invigorated legislature and public opinion, which are beginning to gain access to policy discussion, if not policy decision. As the coalitions of political interest become much more complex, conflicts of interest among different political actors, including different government agencies, become more intense. This in turn opens up new possibilities for sectoral interests to play on these divisions and to exploit them for their own purposes. As a result, presidential influence has been modified by the gradual decrease of absolute control over policy direction. This in itself is the product of the growing influence of bureaucratic and other political actors, popular demands for democratization, and external economic influences, such as natural resource shortages and world financial market adjustments, that lie outside the president's sphere of control. In short, whereas the president used to have absolute control over the policy process, he must increasingly act as a broker between often-conflicting interests among private and public actors.

Rapid industrial and technological progress has also brought new realities to Korean economic development planning. Since the early 1960s, the Korean government has taken an active role in intervening in the economy through industrial policy schemes. Through the early 1980s, emphasis was placed on developing a pattern of industrial development wherein mastery of basic industries was followed sequentially by those of a more complex nature. Past practices relegated technological development as a means of accomplishing manufacturing-oriented ends that would take advantage of Korea's low-wage, but skilled, workforce (Pack and Westphal 1986; Westphal, Kim, and Dahlman 1985). New global market factors suggest that this path of product-oriented development, be it textile, steel, or consumer electronics, will no longer suffice for Korea. Other newly industrializing countries with lower wage rates and equal access to new production practices may marginalize Korea's once-enviable position in the world market. Korea also faces pressure from the United States and the European Community for greater access to Korean markets, just as protectionist tendencies are gaining voice in both North America and Western Europe. To be a viable international competitor, Korea has little choice but to scramble up the ladder of value-added manufacturing. As a result, the Korean government has recently displayed an interest in emphasizing technological innovation as a primary policy goal or concern in the context of economic and industrial development strategies.

In recent years, scholars have begun to distinguish technology policy as a component of general economic development policy schemes. Through technology policy, the state pursues courses of action which facilitate the development of technology and foster its access by sectoral interests (Branscomb 1991). Industrial policy, on the other hand, is more targeted and involves governmental intervention in specific manufacturing and product sectors and is aimed at matching or surpassing similar actions taken by other states or, arguably, to take advantage of the lack of commensurate policy actions among other states. Technology policy involves not only the enhancement of technological capability through encouraging research and development for successful absorption and improvement of imported technologies, but also the development of processes to create and utilize new products and practices (T. Kim 1994; L. Kim and Dahlman 1992). In short, technology policy as a component of general economic planning can be seen as entailing three dimensions: acquiring advanced foreign technology, diffusing imported technology, and developing indigenous technology.

The concept of technological acquisition and application is deeply rooted in the literature on development. The ability of a state to successfully adopt new technology as a means of achieving developmental goals has been viewed as a central tenet in modernization and development theory (for discussion, see Geddes 1991), although its presence in discussion is often more implied than explicit. Ideally, technology can pave the way for enhanced economic activity, improved infrastructure, and advances in the quality of life. Much of the discussions surrounding development have centered on two themes. The first focuses on how to acquire new technologies to assist in economic development strategies. The second focuses on how to control the means of transmission by which technologies are acquired. In the former category, we can place many of the discussions between the relative merits of interventionist and neoclassical approaches to economic development. The latter category has served as a focusing topic for those warning of the implications of dependency on external actors for economic development. In these discussions, concern is not so much geared to the relative measure of success in economic development as to its effect on the societal arrangements in which technologies have been used to structure and influence markets and economy. In the case of Korea, experience illustrates how the state sought to foster technology acquisition to achieve short-term economic development goals and how the conditions evolved to a degree to which the state sought to enhance the longer-term goals of increasing Korea's technological development capacities. This transformation, which we detail in chapter 5, helps to illustrate how industrial policy and technology policy have, in many ways, merged into one policy area.

The growing interrelationship between industrial policy and technology policy to achieve international competitiveness cannot be overemphasized (see Branscomb 1991; Justman and Teubal 1988). Technological advance and industrial application are now seen as key components in an overall economic and industrial policy strategy (see, for example, Graham 1992; Skolnikoff 1993). While this close relationship between the two has also become appreciated in policy circles, preexisting institutional arrangements can serve to catalyze or hinder comprehensive strategies to coordinate industrial and technology policy. How Korea will fare in the face of this new technological policy imperative is yet to be known. But by documenting past practices and current developments in policy-making arrangements for technological innovation, we can at least offer a picture of the landscape in which these new developments will play out.

These factors pose both opportunities and challenges for the presidency and the bureaucracy in Korea. The key element to policy success will rest in the ability to adapt and capitalize on social, economic, and technological changes. We contend that the president-centered model will continue to prevail in Korea. But for it to be successful in meeting future domestic needs, a more adaptive stance will need to be taken. Such a posture will likely involve an embrace of technology development and application policy as a primary component of economic development strategies. Such a stance will probably require the effective involvement of political, bureaucratic, industrial, and research actors in both policy formation and execution. Obviously, such arrangements will place a premium on coordination and cooperation between the executive and the bureaucracy, as well as among bureaucratic actors. Given past Korean industrialization experience in which presidential will has prevailed, these may be difficult objectives to achieve.

In this regard, an analysis of the Korean presidency as it stands at the crossroads of a transition from autocratic arrangements to an increasingly democratic environment can help shed light on the complexity of governmental arrangements in developing states. In particular, examination of presidential priorities and involvement in technology policy in association with broader economic development priorities is appropriate for understanding a developmental state in transition. This transition is the product of the political dynamics of democratization and the substantive complexity of economic development planning schemes aimed at enhancing technological resources and capacities. Therefore, this study can be of importance, considering recent scholastic concerns about the ability of existing theories to explain change in developmental states.

UNDERSTANDING DEVELOPMENTAL TRANSITION: THE KOREAN CASE

Since 1962, Korea has undergone a rapid transition from an agrarian to an advanced technological society. This has been achieved at no small cost, in terms of those values held dear to adherents of democratic institutional arrangements. Korean development, at least through the mid-1980s, was achieved as a result of state policies that imposed controls and direction of the course of economic development that dictated capital flows and allocation, regulated technology transfer from abroad, set priorities for sectoral development, and suppressed consumer demand for the sake of increased industrial capacity. Policy decisions relating to these objectives were arrived at through nondemocratic means, being, as they were, the product of the desires and perspectives of the president and a small circle of advisors. The role of the bureaucracy, which was both mature and highly professionalized, was to function primarily as policy implementor and to serve in a limited advisory capacity. Other governmental institutions, such as the legislature and the courts, were weak and ineffectual in providing a check on presidential prerogative and power. Social institutions such as the press, labor unions, and citizen groups were suppressed by the authoritarian regime.

In the 1980s, a number of forces converged to begin to fray the bonds of authoritarian control. One of the primary forces for change was long-simmering dissent by student and labor groups that boiled over into visible conflict through the 1980s. The key to the influence of these groups in pushing for greater democratization was winning the sympathy of the middle class. The regime of President Chun Doo Hwan crudely reacted to the challenge by means of violent suppression and acts of intimidation which drew attention on the world stage and strengthened resistance at home. Chun was eventually forced to accommodate the popular opposition by accepting direct presidential elections in 1986, leading to his exit from office.

Many observers credit the uprising of students and labor as the key ingredient in sparking democratization in Korea. There is no doubt some justification for this, but one should not be misled to believe that democratization has bloomed full-flower in Korea. Instead, such a transition is more the product of a desire for social liberalization. Under the rubric of social liberalization, democracy is but one of a number of values that are held in high regard. Such scholars as Bell (1973), Inglehart (1977), and Douglas and Wildavsky (1982) have noted how citizens in highly developed (or postindustrial or postmaterial) societies come to focus on quality of life issues that mark a sharp departure from the more immediate demands of securing the necessities of survival. Based on our observations and supplemented by recent studies found in the literature (see Abramson and Inglehart 1995; Lee 1994), we hold that this phenomenon is also happening in postdevelopmental societies.

Ironically, the promise of social liberalization in Korea would not have been possible without economic concessions that were made by the state to entrenched capitalist interests. These concessions severely undermined the government's ability to influence capital financing and industrial development priorities in the marketplace. Once the state lost ground in controlling the marketplace, it lost its dominance over capital. In turn, the utility of the state, in the eyes of capital interests, diminished. No longer was the state necessary as a source of financing, an ally to suppress consumer and labor demands, or a means of providing protection from foreign competition. Instead, the state was seen in some ways as a hindrance to diversification and was increasingly seen more as an avenue of recourse to address discrete or specific concerns rather than as a partner in economic activity. The decline of the state's status in economic affairs has led to its diminished status in the social sphere.

After decades of seeking to describe and explain the nature of developmental states and their political institutions and actors, scholars are now faced with the task of explaining the emergence of what can be termed the postdevelopmental state. The postdevelopmental state is the ironic outcome of rapid economic success which undermines the legitimacy of existing state institutional arrangements. The postdevelopmental state has, in essence, bypassed the way station of the developed state on the road to modernization. From a theoretical standpoint, the developmental state experience has been explained from various perspectives. Apologists of the strong state have portrayed strong executive and peak organization arrangements as necessary for achieving economic progress. From this perspective, social liberalization and more equitable distribution of wealth will be the by-product of achievements in economic development. For others, authoritarian arrangements were seen as allowing entrenched interests to capture resources that might otherwise be used for broader economic development purposes. Two disparate perspectives share this view.

For adherents to neoclassical economics, the presence of an interventionist state hamstrings the workings of efficient market arrangements. For neo-Marxists, such arrangements represent the ability of entrenched elite actors to deny more equitable policy decisions and resource allocations (for discussions, see Colclough 1991; Toye 1991; Evans 1991; Chilcote 1994).

Thus, for the better part of a half-century, the discussion of developmental states has been couched in broad theoretical, and sometimes ideological, terms that have centered on the legitimacy of the strong state as an actor in economic development. In the same breath, the limits of the developmental state in determining the course of development have been open to question—ranging from interpretations which hold that states are mere conduits for the interests of foreign influence to a defense which holds that self-determination and autarky are sovereign rights and the best policy prescription for developing nations. Inherent in most of these discussions, though, has been the assumption that states were modernizing and moving to the status of a developed nation. Ideally, such an eventual achievement would embody not only mature economic markets, whether command or free, that guaranteed effective allocation of wealth and resources, but also well-developed and participatory political environments which embraced individual liberties and institutional counterbalances. Whether this status would be a mirror of existing developed nations or a counterfeit was the subject of conjecture and interpretation based on ideological and theoretical filters.

But in the decades since the end of World War II, the developmental experience played out much differently than prescription and prediction would have it. Far too many states have not even broken free of the starting blocks toward development, existing as impoverished and all too often politically malevolent entities. For a small group of nations who have earned the appellation of newly industrialized countries (NICs), economic development has been great—though often at the expense of social and political liberalization. The economic success of these nations (which include such East Asian countries as Korea and Taiwan, and the city-states of Singapore and Hong Kong) has been, depending on the observer, held up as evidence of the benefits of both neoclassical and interventionist approaches to development. Thus some, like Amsden (1989) and Fallows (1994), laud the manner in which

states have manipulated market arrangements for the greater benefit of national economic development, while others, such as the
World Bank (1993) and Krueger (1979; 1995), have used the experiences of these states to emphasize the importance of liberal and
free-trade arrangements.

The problem with much of the examination of the developmental state is that it has all too often been limited to discussions
that center on economic performance. Broad macroeconomic indicators often become the benchmarks of success on the road to
modernization and progress. Commentators are sometimes enam-
ored with the success stories of late modernizers, newly industrialized countries, and the like. Given that economic success is often
easily seen as a surrogate of democratic and participatory institutional development, the question of the social costs of such
achievements is sometimes ignored. However, when discussions
shift from economics to politics, the scope of survey is all too
often limited to general discussions about the relative positions
and relationships between such ambiguous and amorphous group-
ings as the state, capital, and labor in developing states. In these
discussions, there is the risk that the more complex interrelation-
ships among and within institutional and societal arrangements
will be overlooked or not given adequate treatment in analysis.
Such interpretation is bound to be one-dimensional and lacking
in understanding of the subtle interplay and change that may
take place in relationships between key political and societal
actors.

THE EMERGENCE OF THE POSTDEVELOPMENTAL STATE

An understanding of the complexities of institutional makeup
and arrangements is a key tool in identifying and interpreting the
rise of the postdevelopmental state. This is particularly important
because one of the traits of the postdevelopmental state is the
change in power differentials among government institutions and
between government institutions and private or sectoral interests.
Here, the case of Korea is very illustrative. As we will see, the presidency, long the driving institutional force in Korean government,
is undergoing a transformation. A greater emphasis is placed on
the brokering skills of presidents, as judged in their terms, to
mediate conflict between contending interests, both within and

outside of government, and on their ability to build the coalitions necessary to achieve agenda and policy objectives.

The changing role of the state vis-a-vis other institutions and actors, such as business and labor interests, signifies another crucial dimension of the postdevelopmental state. In the case of Korea, we can go so far as to claim that the state is beginning to exhibit signs of an identity crisis. For the postdevelopmental state, a crisis of legitimacy and identity may occur—one which is beyond the type of regime or arrangement in power and is grounded in the twin forces of social legitimacy and efficacy. In terms of the former, there is the new expectation that constitutionalism and institutionalism will replace political power arrangements based on strength of personality and tools of coercion. In terms of the latter, the ability of the state to influence economic outcomes has diminished, as compared to the prevailing dominance once enjoyed through comprehensive economic and industrial development programs.

The postdevelopmental state may be evaluated by the changes that occur within its internal sphere, in terms of institutional arrangements and relationships with major societal and economic actors. But examination of the external relationships with foreign actors is also requisite, especially to understand the role that economic growth and industrialization plays in the transformation of society. The relationship between the state and external influences has been the primary theoretical underpinning in the examination of the developmental experience (for discussions, see Chilcote 1994; Geddes 1991). It should also serve as an anchor for discussions of the postdevelopmental state. A thumbnail sketch of the postdevelopmental state requires an overview of identifying relevant political, social, and economic characteristics. These can best be illustrated in outlining some of the possible conditions and changes that state, society, and markets will face and undergo.

Diminished influence of the state over social and economic activity will be one of the primary characteristics of the postdevelopmental state. The power of the state will be constrained by forces both internal and external to the institutional arrangements that make up government. Internally, the requirement for strong executives to share power and responsibility with other institutional actors, such as the courts, the legislature, and local governments, will likely result in cross-cutting and contradictory policy and program arrangements. Coherence and coordination, often associated with strong-executive arrangements, will likely fade in the face of more dynamic policy arrangements which will influence agenda-setting, policy formulation, and implementation.

Such a transition to shared institutional power is bound be less than smooth. Indeed, one of the greatest challenges facing the postdevelopmental state is the chore of accommodating pluralistic interests with what can only be termed *immature* political institutions. The capacity of legislatures, parties, and local governments to provide forums for expression, a means of representation, and venues for policy action is uncertain. As we will see in the case of Korea, the major institutions of government are undergoing profound change. For example, the Korean legislature has become more activist in recent years, primarily as a venue for competing factions to voice concerns and policy preferences. The courts have recently emerged as key players in efforts to bring past acts of political corruption and suppression to justice. Added to this is the role played by local governments in Korea, which now enjoy greater independence from the national government. There will also be challenges to achieving effective social participation and the arrangements necessary for democratization. The ability of transitory, candidate-centered parties to become enduring political organizations will be just one of the major tests facing democratization and social liberalization in Korea.

Change in the postdevelopmental state will be more than the transition to power and responsibilities shared among institutions of the state. Government will also have to wrestle with the reality that the power of the state has diminished in relationship to major economic players in the economy. As we will see in Korea, for example, the growth of business conglomerates, or *chaebols*, has reached the point at which business interests enjoy substantial autonomy from what the state might desire. Increasingly, these actors are seeking to determine their own priorities, to access their own sources of capital for expansion, and to interact independently in the global marketplace (for discussions, see Steers, Shin, and Ungson 1989; Fields 1995). The ability of capital interests to outstrip the state's ability to control investment patterns, trade arrangements, and spillover effects may pose major challenges to the postdevelopmental state.

The relative independence of domestic capital interests is one external force shaping the postdevelopmental state; another has to do with the nature of international trade in the global market-place. The past two decades have seen an intensification of agreements and treaties involving international trade and market access. In order to become a player in these markets, developing states have been pressured to relinquish some policy controls over their economies (see Krueger 1995; Ostry and Nelson 1995). In the postdevelopmental state, we can expect this trend to continue. The presence of multinational actors in the domestic economy, either in the form of national firms reaching across boundaries or due to the presence of foreign firms, will no doubt amplify pressures for states to be more outward-looking and accommodating to the needs of international capital interests.

Finally, the postdevelopmental state may suffer a general crisis of legitimacy in the societal arena. A level of alienation among large segments of the population because of their economic prospects in times of uncertainty and change is to be expected. In Korea, this has been manifested in a sense of discord regarding the legitimacy of the current government, relations with the United States, and the future course of Korean national development, especially in regard to reunification policy.

In the chapters that follow, we will outline the dynamics of the developmental state experience in Korea and how this newly industrialized country is on the threshold of postdevelopmental status. We will examine this transformation by focusing on the role of the presidency and the bureaucracy through a conceptual filter that clarifies the effect of structural and rational-choice perspectives on presidential and bureaucratic behavior. Our examination will focus primarily on activities relating to technology policy. Technology policy serves as an excellent vehicle to chart relationships between the president and bureaucracy and the policy priorities and objectives associated with efforts to promote economic and industrial development. Further, though not always obviously stated, technology policy, because of its association with foreign trade and intervention in the markets of developing countries and because it is used as a measure of self-sufficiency, has long been a part of analyses in the developmental literature.

POLICY ARRANGEMENTS AS A FOCUS OF STUDY

Understanding the dynamics of transition in the developmental state is a challenging enterprise. As we will argue, this can best be achieved by the use of interpretive frameworks which allow an analysis of conditions and events shaping the activities of policy makers and the interests and motives of the policy makers themselves. But such analysis also needs to be made manageable by focusing on a critical theme or topic of study in relationship to the developmental state experience. Judging from the focus given on trade policy in the literature on comparative economic and political systems, this appears to be well-understood. For our part, we have decided to focus on technology policy in general, and specifically on those policies dealing with technology transfer, to provide an exploration of the developmental state in transition. In the case of Korea, technology-oriented policy is an effective vehicle of analysis because it stands at the nexus of policies and objectives relating to industrialization, capacity building, trade, and modernization. In addition, due to the complexities of the subject, it is a policy area that has seen considerable interaction between presidents and their bureaucratic advisors. Finally, Korea's experience with technology policy helps to illustrate how the developmental state grapples with the dynamic conditions of global markets and international relations.

Specifically, with regard to technological development in Korea, the dependence approach argues that technological and industrial acquisition and adoption, particularly foreign investments, can lead to rapid economic growth in developing nations. At the same time, it also warns of the dangers of dominance, namely foreign control of the domestic market, absence of domestic production ownership, and exploration of the host country's surpluses (see Evans 1979; O'Donnell 1973; for detailed discussions, see Haggard 1990; Mardon 1990). Such dominance can hamper effective economic development and disrupt the social fabric of the development state. This perspective assumes the dominant influence of the donor country over the developing host country. However, this dependence perspective had not predicted and could not explain Korean industrialization and technology-transfer policy, in which foreign investments have been minimal and have not been the primary beneficiary of economic growth. Also, domestic markets have not been strongly dominated by any foreign firms or multinational corporations (see Mardon 1990).

According to the neoclassical approach, foreign investments and advanced technology are positive forces that lead to industrial growth; it implicitly assumes the strong influence of the donor country on the industrialization patterns of a developing host country. This perspective has found favor in many circles, especially in the international development community (see World Bank 1993). However, as we noted earlier, such a perspective ignores the highly active role that the host country's government policy can play in comprehensive technological development planning and the strict regulation of foreign investments and technology inflows (Johnson 1987; Mardon 1990; Wade 1992). This has certainly been the case in Korea, and the neoclassical approach simply cannot fully explain the country's industrial development and technology-transfer policy led by high levels of strong state guidance over primary economic and industrial activities (Mardon 1990).

In contrast to the neoclassical explanation, the developmental state approach ascribes Korea's successful industrial development to strong, but deliberate, state guidance over targeting of selected industries for technological development. This strategy concentrates on the sector's development for a preplanned period by assimilating foreign technologies to assist development and lead to sophisticated industries and technologies (see Amsden 1989; Deyo 1987; Haggard and Moon 1990; Johnson 1982, 1987; Jones and Sakong 1980; Mardon 1990; Wade 1990, 1992; White 1988). In contrast to the dependence and neoclassical approaches, this developmental perspective argues for the strong influence of the host country's policy on its technological development and patterns of technology transfer. However, as we noted earlier, the developmental state approach tends to overlook the dynamics of state influence over economic development. One reason for this is that it often neglects the importance of technological innovation as a factor in development (Wade 1992; Bernard and Ravenhill 1995).

With the current pattern of technological development, Korea has begun to reflect generalizations that the modern state is now the agent of a coalition of interests, which may vary from issue to issue (Hart 1992). Therefore, the state must confer extensively with other social actors in order to affect a change in industrial policies. This is a new understanding of the role of the state in regard to the Korean technological development policy and its technology-transfer strategy. The emerging literature implies that the very same features of the government technology-transfer policy that until the late 1980s were conducive for the rapid expansion of Korea's export-led industrialization now have become constraints for attempts to sustain industrialization through technology-transfer arrangements (Ernst 1994; Hahm, Plein, and Florida, 1994). Therefore, examination of state involvement in technology-transfer policy, particularly foreign investments in association with broader economic development priorities, is appropriate for understanding the dynamics of the developmental state in transition.

CONCLUSION

As developmental states have matured to a level where government control over social and economic development is unclear, established frameworks of analysis have lost much of their explanatory power. The emergence of, and prospects for, the postdevelopmental state invite investigation and inquiry. We argue that state-specific studies can make a contribution to such research. Korea is a particularly useful model for study because it is now on the threshold of postdevelopmental status. The decline of authoritarian arrangements and corresponding democratization, the economic transformation which sees a greater independence for market actors from the state, and the uncertain prospects for the future in political and social terms are all hallmarks of the contemporary Korean experience. As we have outlined in this chapter, the complexities of this experience can be investigated through policy and institutional specific analysis—namely the study of the presidency and bureaucracy in regard to various aspects of technology policy. In order to capture the influence that history and current conditions have had on the decisions and perspectives of the presidency and bureaucracy, it is necessary to construct a framework that considers both structural influence and the choices and actions that individual political actors are allowed to take. It is to such a framework that we turn in the following chapter.

3

An Interpretative Framework for the Korean Presidency and Bureaucracy

Since the early 1960s, the Korean government has taken an active role in the country's impressive economic and industrial development. However, rapid economic progress has also brought new realities to the authoritarian structure of the Korean presidency and bureaucracy and their nexus. New presidential arrangements (characterized by real fixed terms and democratic accountability), brought on by the initiation of political democratization and economic internationalization, have diminished the absolute influence of the president over the bureaucracy and the bureaucracy over other social and business actors and policy control. This institutional change contributes to bureaucratic fragmentation and conflicts, leading to "turf wars" among cabinet ministries. As a result, bureaucratic arrangements have lost their effectiveness as streamlined and cohesive instruments of policy development and implementation. The state is consequently seen more as an impediment to, rather than a vehicle for, industrial and economic progress. Yet, in spite of the overall decrease in policy influence over social and economic matters, given an authoritarian tradition in Korean politics, in an era of social and political democratization and economic internationalization, the executive–bureaucratic nexus will likely remain the primary locus of the continued economic and industrial progress.

Despite the salience and perceived importance of executive–bureaucratic arrangements, however, there is little consensus in the literature regarding the underlying factors that might explain the decline of the state, particularly the authoritarian executive–bureaucratic nexus, in policy control. This is due, in part, to a tendency in the literature on development to take a broad sociological view of change in contemporary Korea (see Jacobs 1985; Cumings 1987; Evans 1987; Koo 1987, 1990; Johnson 1987).

30

While effective in portraying the scope of change, these approaches are limited when it comes to examining the institutional dimensions of the decline of authoritarian arrangements in Korea.

We assert that the rise and decline of authoritarian executive–bureaucratic arrangements in Korea can be effectively assessed through the use of an interpretive framework which combines elements of structural determinism (see, for example, Lipset 1959; Inglehart 1977; Burkhart and Lewis-Beck 1994) and rational-choice perspectives (see, for example, Harsanyi 1969; Monroe 1991). From the latter, we are able to examine and interpret specific executive and bureaucratic motives and perspectives, based on analyses of specific policy actions and positions. From the former, we are able to understand how various conditions have shaped the institutions and parameters in which political and bureaucratic activity play out. By combining a structuralist and rationalist approach, we can understand the different conditions, constraints, and stimuli that prompt individual action and decisions. Such an approach helps to illustrate how political and bureaucratic actors comprehend opportunities and how these options are time-bound—thus allowing a clearer understanding of the strategic behavior of these political and bureaucratic actors within a changing environment (see Casper and Taylor 1996; Kohno 1992). Applied here, such a perspective offers an explanation of why Korean development has not followed a course postulated by modernization theorists whose work is based on models of structural determinism. Further, such a perspective throws light on the internal dynamics and tensions between executive leaders and bureaucratic actors in authoritarian states.

In sum, we find that a combination of structural forces and the changing conditions which serve as rational-expectation rewards and consequences served to make both the rise of the authoritarian state possible and its demise inevitable. For regime leaders (i.e., presidents and their inner circle of advisors), the absolute distinction between power and the consequences of its loss in the face of challenges from within and outside of government led to short-term decisions that alienated key societal actors and powers. The Korean case also shows that regime leaders focused intensely on export-driven economic growth as a means of maintaining legitimacy. In short, we find that the short-term horizons present in rational-choice decisions work against the prospects of ordered and rational long-term policy goals—even in highly centralized systems, such as the authoritarian regimes that existed in Korea for some thirty years.

In order to present our framework and interpretation of the Korean experience, this chapter is organized in the following manner. First we provide a brief review of the foundations of our approach, including an outline of the basic elements of the structural–rational perspective. Second, we present an historical overview of the emergence of the authoritarian executive–bureaucratic arrangement. We then turn our discussion to describe how institutional arrangements have changed in the face of social and political democratization and economic internationalization. Finally, we conclude with a brief discussion of the future prospects of new bureaucratic politics to cope with social and political democratization and economic internationalization.

BUILDING THE FRAMEWORK: STRUCTURAL AND RATIONAL CHOICE FOUNDATIONS

Analysis of the state often occurs on one of two levels. In one dimension, focus is given to the broad structural elements that help determine a state's destiny. For example, modernization theory postulates a series of deterministic stages outlining the social and economic development. Such a deterministic approach has found resonance in a wide array of treatments of developmental state experiences. These broad-scale approaches often entail comparisons and examinations of the relationships between three broadly defined elements of society: the state, capital, and labor (Hart 1992; Im 1990; E. Kim 1994). The other dimension of analysis tends to focus on individual participation in the political arena, be it as a leader, bureaucrat, legislator, or citizen. From this perspective, attention is given to the motives, rationales, and strategies utilized by actors in the give and take of politics. Broadly speaking, macroanalysis that focuses on the evolution and dynamics of state experiences often has a structural or deterministic dimension associated with historical conditions and contemporary events. Conversely, analysis of the behaviors of specific individuals in the policy arena often tends to focus on their independence as self-interested or rational actors.

Much of the literature on the developmental state tends to concentrate on a triad of principal actors whose level of interaction and relationships determines the course of economic and social development. This triad consists of the state, often described as a self-interested actor; capital, which is comprised of both domestic capitalist elites and foreign corporate interests; and labor, which is seen as the agitating force for more equitable resource allocation and the champion of the public welfare. These general categories provide a useful organizing device for discussion and inquiry. However, like other broad taxonomies, they leave something to be desired when we want to concentrate on specifics, say on the experience of one country or the experience of one of these actors. Indeed, the literature of the role of the Korean state in economic development tends to underplay the complexities of its executive–bureaucratic arrangements and relationships. The focus of the literature has primarily been on the dynamics of the relationship between the state and capital, and how the two, particularly the state, have reacted to the growing presence of labor as the third developmental state actor (Im 1987; Kim 1994; Amsden 1989; Bedeski 1994).

The need to get a better sense of what comprises the state as a collection of self-interested actors has become the focus of much scholarly inquiry (Clark and Chan 1994; Evans, Rueschemeyer, and Skocpol 1985; Haggard 1990; Haggard and Moon 1990; Johnson 1987; D. Kang 1995; Mitchell 1991; Moon and Prasad 1994; Nordlinger 1981; Wade 1990, 1992; Rockman 1990). In some guises, this line of research has been referred to as the *new institutionalism*, though *state-centered political economy* is perhaps a better descriptor where such policies dealing with economic development, industrialization, and technology are the focus (Geddes 1991). But this process of separation and categorization can fall short by failing to unbundle the various actors that make up the state—especially in those states that can be characterized as developmental–authoritarian. Indeed, the greatest risk of misperception takes form in the notion of a monolith whose purposes are defined and whose course is set by strict hierarchical, if not authoritarian, control.

Because of failure to see distinctions within the state, depictions of the experiences of developmental–authoritarian states, such as Korea, have tended to stress the strong, determined role of the state. Such characterizations give a flavor of concerted efforts that are the product of rigid hierarchies and strong bureaucratic compliance to policy directives. But by moving beyond the veil from which we have defined the state, we can see how the internal tensions, relationships, and arrangements within the state display insights on the developmental–authoritarian state. In the Korean experience, by decoupling the president and his inner circle from administrative arrangements, we can note the internal tensions that make up the dynamics of executive–bureaucratic relationships. This can best be achieved through the analytical perspective of the structural–rational approach.[1]

Such a perspective, which takes into account the constraints, orientations, and behavior patterns of institutional players, is reminiscent of theories of bureaucratic decision making advanced by Simon (1947), Allison (1969), and Bendor and Moe (1984). These and similar approaches are implicitly built upon rational-choice perspectives but are clearly attuned to the influence of organizational culture on bureaucratic activity. The scope of contextual factors influencing behavior can be expanded to involve larger social and historical factors as well. This has been something of an ideal in rational-choice theory and has deep roots (see Harsanyi 1969), but has yet to be satisfactorily achieved. In recent years, scholars have reiterated the importance of combining rational-choice perspectives with structuralist conditions (see Monroe 1991; Ostrom 1991).

The rational-choice perspective is based on methodological individualism and assumes that individuals can compare expected benefits and costs of actions prior to adopting strategies for action (see Ostrom 1991). Therefore, it implicitly assumes that institutional constraints are exogenous in the sense that all political and bureaucratic actors must take legal and political constraints as "givens" in making actual individual choices. Therefore, political and bureaucratic actors will seek to maximize their benefits under set institutional rules and expectations, be they the product of laws, regulations, or norms (Kohno 1992:382). While they provide a set of given parameters, the rules themselves are not beyond change in terms of interpretation or application (Ostrom 1991; Wilson 1995). As Kohno (1992) noted, within established institutional frameworks, there exists a great deal of uncertainty. Indeed, the experience of bureaucratic politics is noted for shifting objectives and particular strategies and tactics tailored for circumstances and effect.

In essence, the institutional environment in which individual actions and decisions are carried out is a loosely fixed and dynamic arena. Unfortunately, the rational-choice perspective, by dint of execution and purpose, is often driven to assume static givens and outcomes. To execute modeling, assumptions are often fixed. Most importantly, the ideal of equilibrium is a static concept. This is unfortunate and unnecessary. It is unfortunate in the sense that the rational-choice perspective was championed early as an alternative explanatory model for what were deemed static structural–functionalist models of political development in the comparative context (Harsanyi 1969:514). It is unnecessary in the sense that dynamic assumptions can be incorporated into the rational-choice perspective through the incorporation of the more dynamic concepts of social change and human agency (see Monroe 1991; Ostrom 1991), though methodological execution through mathematical modeling may prove difficult.

The structural–rational approach developed here builds on existing efforts to understand the combined effect of deterministic environmental influences and the latitude of individual choice in the process of policy making and institutional control. Such a perspective has been identified as a theoretical framework (see Ostrom 1991) and in different forms has been applied to the study of authoritarian states (see Kasza 1987), the power of private enterprise in developing states (see Fields 1995), and regime changes (for a discussion, see Kitschelt 1992).[2] Kasza's description of the combined effect of these forces is instructive. Describing bureaucratic arrangements in authoritarian states, he notes:

> Bureaucratic policy making is strongly influenced by external factors such as historical circumstances, cultural values, and the impact of other social institutions. Organizational structures themselves contain a complex potpourri of stimuli that can sway individual behavior and collective action in contradictory ways. As important as it is to understand the impact of these structures, structures alone merely offer opportunities for social action. At every step, the decisions made by human beings as to how they will use those opportunities are critical to the policy-making process, and these decisions are made in large part free of structural determination (Kasza 1987:869).

In our formulation of the approach, we give emphasis to two dimensions of political activity that the structural–rationalist perspective can help illuminate. The first dimension deals with institutional focus. In our analysis, we concentrate on the relationships between the political executive and the bureaucracy. In this sense, we are dismantling the developmental–authoritarian state to look at its most relevant parts. The second dimension deals with time and its effects on the strength of structural influence and on the strategies of policy actors. A perspective that charts behavior and response over time allows us to document how changing conditions alter the structure of decision and action. In short, we can document how, as the mixture of factors changes over time, so does the nature of executive and bureaucratic behavior.

INTERPRETING THE EMERGENCE AND EVOLUTION OF AUTHORITARIAN ARRANGEMENTS

The specific historical and cultural experiences of a state provide its own unique institutional and policy arrangements (Hofferbert 1974; Ashford 1992). For example, according to Geddes (1991), bureaucratic authoritarianism is the product of state-led responses to actual and perceived threats from domestic and external sources, such as the threat of communism, stiff international competition, and military defense concerns. Geddes (1991:54) notes:

> This convergence of interests provides the basis of a coalition of the domestic bourgeoisie, the international bourgeoisie [e.g. multi-national corporations], and the state dominated by the military and technocrats, which supports the bureaucratic–authoritarian regime and its policies. The bureaucratic–authoritarian argument thus offers an explanation for why several of the more advanced developing countries succumbed to authoritarianism when modernization theory would have predicted that further development would make democracy more likely.

Modernization theory refers to a deterministic perspective which holds that economic development will bring social gains that are manifested in democratic practices and a general commitment to equity in the liberty to participate in market arrangements. In attempting to pull together a cohesive body of literature, researchers are made to advance generalizations regarding various types of arrangements. But as we move to the study of specific state arrangements, it is useful again to identify the unique forces that have brought about the evolution of the state. Korea's rapid economic advances through the 1970s made it a prime candidate for such achievements. But conditions put such realizations on hold, as the state balked at reform measures that would strengthen the hand of labor and by extension of the masses, at the perceived risk of derailing Korea's export-oriented development plans which relied on the suppression of wages and fiscal policies beneficial to capital interests. The emergence of a strong state, which was a powerful agent of social, political, and economic change, was deeply influenced by historical and contemporary events.

Cultural, social, economic, and political conditions placed constraints and parameters on the evolution of the authoritarian state. The individual strategies employed by the regimes of presidents Park, Chun, and Rho, and bureaucratic responses to the imposition of presidentially imposed policy imperatives, helped to define the developmental experience. The rational-expectation strategies of regime leadership tended to focus on absolutist strategies aimed at securing and maintaining primacy. The rational-expectation behavior of bureaucratic actors was characterized primarily by responses to a very narrow and powerful range of principals.

Structural Influences and Factors:
History and the Developmental Imperative

A brief sketch of the rise of the Korean authoritarian state demonstrates the rise of a strong president-based system whose organizing principle was to transform an agrarian society into a modern industrialized state. Certain conditions shaped how this evolution unfolded. First, given its past colonization by Japan, Korean development evidenced a desire to minimize foreign dominance of the economic sector (Mardon 1990; E. Kim 1994). Second, the threat of North Korea and the Cold War environment put Korea on a defensive footing that allowed preferential treatment by the United States in trade matters. Third, in order to maintain legitimacy and to manage the complexities of economic development strategies capably, the Korean presidency established, and increasingly came to rely upon, bureaucratic arrangements dealing with such areas as finance, industrialization, and technology policy (Cheng 1990; Mardon 1990; Hahm and Plein 1995; Wade 1992). Together these conditions and forces helped to facilitate the emergence of strong authoritarian executive–bureaucratic arrangements. In short, the dynamic relationship that emerged between military dictatorship and authoritarian bureaucracy or between political authority and bureaucratic expertise (Chung 1989) contributed to successful export-oriented economic and industrial development.

The emergence of strong authoritarian executive–bureaucratic arrangements can be traced back to the assumption of power by General Park Chung Hee through a coup in 1961.[3] Given his nondemocratic path to the presidency, Park sought to instill and build legitimacy through intensive economic development schemes based on export-oriented production (see E. Kim 1994; Haggard and Kaufman 1995). To do so required instilling a sense of public confidence and support for the regime and its policy aims. This feat was no easy task, given the fact that the centerpiece of the economic growth strategy required a suppressed wage base and deferred benefits to labor. During the early years of Korea's industrialization, its chief attribute of comparative advantage was cheap, but well-motivated and -trained, labor. Those agents who controlled capital also had to defer to the regime's agenda. Through the control of credit, foreign direct investment, and foreign aid, the government was able to pick and choose those firms and sectors slated for growth and expansion (see Steers, Shin, and Ungson 1989; E. Kim 1994).[4]

In the 1960s and 1970s, the Korean government could be regarded as a typical authoritarian developmental state. As described by Watanuki (1995), the state displayed two key characteristics of the developmental state: (1) an effective state apparatus and (2) a strong connection to capital interests, especially with *chaebols*, at the expense of social liberalization. Through the development of economic planning ministries, such as the Economic Planning Board (EPB)[5] and the Ministry of Finance, and the effective control of investment capital, the Park regime was able to determine in large part the course of economic development. In short, the state was the dominant player in relationships with capital interests. These gains were consolidated over time because the Park regime was able to further centralize control over policy direction while allowing for the growth of bureaucracy.

Initially, the assassination of President Park in 1979 gave an indication of a breakdown of, or challenge to, the strong authoritarian state. But his successor, Chun Doo Hwan, amplified authoritarian practices through a series of controversial policy reform actions (see Chung and Jun 1991, for details). The regime's pronounced authoritarianism was in large part a reflection of an internal lack of confidence in the regime's viability. Chun's extralegal means of presidential succession and widespread civil unrest both cast doubt on the legitimacy of the regime. As argued by Cotton (1992), the Chun regime was faced with the difficulties of dealing with a far more complex society and international environment than that of the Park regime. Therefore, it was far more difficult for the Chun regime to build a political machine to institutionalize its rule. Chun responded to this difficulty and uncertainty not only by repressing labor and other agents of social liberalization, but also by giving concessions to capital interests.

In its pursuit of short-term success in quelling social disturbances and maintaining primacy, the Chun regime eroded its own long-term prospects. In 1980, policies were put into place that abolished press freedoms and severely limited labor rights to unionization and dispute-settlement procedures (Oh 1994). This hard-line stance alienated both the working class and the middle class, severely undercutting the Chun regime's basis for legitimacy. In cultivating the support of the business sector, the Chun regime was so accommodating to capital interests that the state lost its ability to function as a predominant actor in setting the course of Korea's economic development. The Chun regime saw dramatic changes in the relationship between the state and capital, as the government sought to broaden its base of support by facilitating the entry of small and medium-size firms into the market. In general, the Chun regime reconfigured the way in which the government dealt with the economy.

Some of the most important changes in the state's relationship to the business sector were manifested in the area of investment and financing. Through the 1980s, the government backed away from its emphasis on heavy industry development, thus freeing up capital for smaller and less resource demanding initiatives. Most importantly, the government diminished its function in the allocation of credit to specific firms. In turn, this action required companies to turn to stock offerings and borrowing on the open market as sources of capital. Furthermore, the government exited the banking business by selling off its stake in commercial banks. Prior to these actions, the government was the majority stockholder in domestic banks, giving it the power to appoint management, set policy, and control loans. Through control of the Bank of Korea and the Ministry of Finance, the government was able to set interest rates (Steers, Shin, and Ungson 1989). This retreat from dominance changed the balance of power between the state and business interests, leading in essence to an identity crisis for the state in the face of uncertainty over its diminishing relevance in economic affairs.

The turmoil of the Chun regime was also reflected in presidential and bureaucratic relations. In the early stages of the Chun presidency, there was an extensive reform and reduction both in top bureaucratic positions and in the number of central government agencies in order to control the bureaucracy (Chung and Jun 1991). Although the state dominated politics, the Chun regime was closely associated with the market for sustaining economic and industrial progress. The state was the main gatekeeper of the market order. In this sense, Korean authoritarianism under the Chun regime can be called market authoritarianism (Im 1995), in which the market was opened but the politics was closed. Relying more on market mechanisms for economic development, however, the Chun regime found its capacity to build an organized base of support diminished.

In sum, the structuralist perspective helps to explain the environmental parameters by which the modern Korean state evolved. Structural conditions—such as the threat of North Korea, the need to transform the economy from its agrarian base, and a tolerant posture toward Korea from the United States in economic policy and ruling regime practices—all contributed to conditions conducive to the emergence of authoritarian executive–bureaucratic arrangements. Structural conditions provided the context, but did not determine the course of events in Korea. As we turn to a rational-choice perspective on bureaucratic and regime behavior, we can see how these conditions helped to shape the context in which individual policy actor choices emerged and played out.

Individual Motives: Regime Survival and Bureaucratic Interests

Although claims could be made that the threat of North Korea necessitated a military regime, the Park regime understood the limitation of such a position and sought legitimacy through the creation of industrial development-oriented bureaucratic arrangements and a results-oriented economic growth policy. Therefore, political survival was dependent on economic development through export-led economic growth (Cheng 1990; Cotton 1992; Wade 1992; Haggard and Kaufman 1995). To achieve this, Park and his successors strengthened the hand of bureaucrats. The bureaucracy was treated as a political tool for sustaining and securing the legitimacy of ruling power, the so-called "Migdal effect." This refers to the tendency of insecurely established leaders to restrain the arms of the bureaucracy in order to prevent challenges to their rule from centers of power within the state, while at the same time relying on those arms for policy effectiveness and legitimacy (Wade 1992). As a result, the executive–bureaucratic relationships tended to be very linear and characteristic of strong principal–agent relationships.

The creation of bureaucratic arrangements was critical to the success and legitimacy of the Park regime. From a symbolic standpoint, bureaucratic agencies could serve as a buffer between the president and capital interests. One of the rationales for the 1961 coup was that the previous regime had been too closely tied with capital interests; Park could hardly risk such claims being made again (E. Kim 1994). From a substantive standpoint, the Park regime needed to have in place a cadre of skilled bureaucrats and administrators to provide information and advice for policy formulation and the skills to implement policy decisions. In the 1960s, the Korean government sought to build up a merit-based bureaucracy, which became firmly established in the early 1970s.

Policy controls placed a great demand on expertise and knowledge, thus giving an advantage to bureaucratic actors immersed in these tasks. Such entities as the Economic Planning Board, the Ministry of Finance, and to a lesser extent the Ministry of Trade and Industry emerged to play important roles in policy planning, development, and implementation (Mardon 1990). Yet, through the 1960s and early 1970s, the presidency continued to set the agenda and course of policy direction. For example, against the Economic Planning Board's recommendations and warnings, the Park administration embarked upon an ill-timed heavy industrialization program during the early 1970s which ultimately slowed Korean economic development considerably (Hahm and Plein 1995). This episode displayed how political expediency and not strategic planning dictated the course of policy development and selection. The argument can be made that the Park regime was seeking to shore up the support of capital interests through massive investment schemes in the face of social resistance to policies to keep wage rates low and through the government's lack of attention toward equitable resource distribution.[6] An outcome of this period of instability was the emergence of strong authoritarian executive–bureaucratic arrangements. Under this authoritarian orientation, coercive measures were used to maintain social order and mobilize national resources, thereby achieving each regime's political goals. This practice dominated through the military regimes of presidents Park, Chun, and even Roh (Jun and Yoon 1995).

Another key feature of this executive–bureaucratic arrangement was that all the power was excessively concentrated in the president (Han 1995). This was certainly the case in the Park and Chun regimes, where presidents exercised dictatorial powers and relied upon personal allies in the highest echelons of government to secure implementation of policy directives (Hahm and Plein 1995). This likely helped the administration increase efficiency; bureaucrats, once they received an order from the top, mobilized all the available resources to achieve the goal as soon as possible. However, this efficiency was so narrowly conceived that it brought about many malfunctions and side effects that did not serve society or economy.[7]

Under the Park and Chun regimes, the lines of control and the scope of principal–agent relationships were clearly drawn. Bureaucrats did not experience the divided loyalties that are often found in those states where other political institutions and organized interests are able to exercise influence. For example, during the authoritarian period, the Korean National Assembly was a very weak institution, political parties were underdeveloped, and interest groups were largely powerless or patronized by the government. Given the rather circumscribed scope of bureaucratic activity and rewards such as prestige, job security, promotion possibilities, and salary and related remunerations during the Park and Chun regimes, the executive–bureaucratic nexus achieved a high level of coordination and effectiveness in advancing export-driven policy initiatives.

INTERPRETING THE DECLINE OF AUTHORITARIAN ARRANGEMENTS

Ironically, the authoritarian executive–bureaucratic arrangement that produced rapid growth also planted the seeds for its own decline (for discussions, see Park 1991; Koo 1993b; Han 1995). Two important by-products of economic development, namely social and political democratization and economic liberalization and globalization, appeared to have hastened the developmental state's reduction of influence in Korean society and economy. The regime transition was the outcome of conflicts among key political actors who were constrained, although not in a deterministic way, by the change in the Korean social structure. It can be understood as the outcome of strategic choices made by key political actors among alternatives that satisfied structural constraints. As a result, a weakening state with social and political democratization and economic liberalization contributed to the decline of the authoritarian executive–bureaucratic nexus. Korea is now in the midst of social and political democratic transition and economic and industrial restructuring. Social and political democratization and general economic liberalization and internationalization have given rise to trade unionism, greater economic independence of big business interests, and the emergence of a more activist press which expresses popular criticism and concern for government policies. At the same time, big business interests have enjoyed greater independence with the retreat of government from investment and credit control.

The authoritarian executive–bureaucratic nexus faced not only mounting social pressure from capital and labor but also other factors as well. One factor concerned growing internal conflict within the state between presidential regimes and the bureaucracy. The other focused on the growing internationalization of Korea's economic sphere. By implication, the consequences of past policy success in economic development have grown to threaten the stability of strong-state arrangements (Evans 1995; E. Kim 1993). Moreover, there is ample evidence that the authoritarian executive–bureaucratic nexus is no longer an effective agent for the realization of national goals (Hahm and Plein 1995).

Structural Conditions: Social and Political Democratization and Economic Internationalization

Although the authoritarian executive–bureaucratic nexus contributed to Korean economic and industrial development, it has become a major obstacle to coping with the new climate of social democratization and economic liberalization (Jun and Yoon 1995). This new environment reflects a number of socioeconomic consequences. Along with urbanization, deepening of industrial structure, diversification of employment structure, expansion of educational opportunity, and heightening of export composition, the middle class, particularly the new middle class and skilled laborers, has expanded very rapidly (Koo 1990; 1991). The authoritarian executive–bureaucratic nexus helped the economic and industrial transformation that brought new actors into the social arena. Once there, these actors developed their own agendas, reshaping the process of economic and industrial transformation and challenging the authoritarian executive–bureaucratic nexus (Evans 1995).

Democratic transition was widely opened up by popular demonstrations in June 1987; this forced the authoritarian Chun regime to accept the direct presidential election which it had resisted since adoption of the Yushin Constitution in 1972 (Casper and Taylor 1996; Han 1995). There was also an explosion of labor discontent in 1987, as reflected in a record number of labor strikes (E. Kim 1994). The Chun regime had no other choice but to accept it, since the level of danger that would otherwise be unavoidable, between military authoritarianism and the student democratic movement, was too high (Casper and Taylor 1996). The pressure for greater social and political democratization increased under President Roh Tae Woo, the handpicked successor of President Chun.

While citizens largely accepted authoritarian arrangements, there was growing discontent toward the individuals who held the reins of power (see Haggard and Kaufman 1995). There are a number of reasons that this must have been so. Politically, the authoritarian executive–bureaucratic nexus suffered very much from the lack of legitimacy. The degree of repression was so high that even physical freedom, the most fundamental civil right, was threatened to an alarming extent. As a result, the level of public trust was very low. The people saw the executive–bureaucratic nexus as ruling over and above itself rather than providing any service of good quality.

In short, the legitimacy of authoritarian executive and bureaucratic arrangements were undercut as a result of challenges against the state and its marginalization as an effective actor in economic development. The state faced a crisis of legitimacy in the face of opposition from students, organized labor, and, significantly, the middle class. The breakdown of the power and influence held at the nexus of presidential and administrative arrangements was not because of failure in economic policy but ironically because of the socioeconomic consequences of policy success (see Han 1995, for details). Im (1995) observes that authoritarian actors had to withdraw from power because the strong state's mission of economic development had been achieved and the purposes of such authority were now moot. Others have argued that Korea's authoritarian leaders have been successful in negotiating their withdrawal from power while preserving influence over the affairs of the state (see Haggard and Kaufman 1995). Those occupying positions in the executive–bureaucratic nexus had little choice but to reconsider their positions in Korean government and politics. Within a climate of successful economic development gains, growing independence of capital interests, and widespread public skepticism about the efficacy and legitimacy of historic governmental arrangements, the question of the obsolescence of the authoritarian state came to the fore. The new political agenda, shaped by calls for policies to address the needs of civil liberties and the public welfare, emphasized the importance of more democratized governmental arrangements. In short, the trend toward liberalization was not limited to economy but expanded to such areas as environment, civic culture, and other quality of life issues.

From a theoretical standpoint, much attention has been given to the influence of labor and other forces of social liberalization and its effect on the transformation of the Korean state (Casper and Taylor 1996; Han 1995; Im 1990, 1995). But to understand the most powerful tides of change, we should look to the changing relationship between the state and capital. The capacity of the state has diminished in the face of the growing economic dominance of successful capital interests. Social liberalization, if it occurs, is arguably more a by-product of market liberalization than an independent force of change. It is not, as we might ideally wish, in itself the engine of political change in authoritarian–bureaucratic systems, such as Korea. Recent developments in the relationship between the state and capital lend credence to this interpretation. In essence, as the size of Korea's economy has grown and dominance of key sectors by *chaebols* has increased, the capacity of the state to influence economic development and outcomes has diminished. By 1984, the combined sales of the top ten *chaebols* represented 67.4 percent of Korea's gross national product (Amsden 1989:116). For example, industries have become increasingly independent in research and development activities, a function once highly dependent on the state (see Hahm and Plein 1995). In the area of the regulation of foreign direct investment, the Korean government has found that the span of policy controls has been diminished due to new technological developments in product and process development (see Hahm, Plein, and Florida 1994).

The liberalization and internationalization of the economy has weakened the ability of the authoritarian executive–bureaucratic arrangement to manage the macroeconomy within its territory. The state has become less able to protect business interests by insulating capital and labor from foreign competitors. The realization of the limits of the state and the pressures brought forth by global competition may well contribute to criticisms of the state and, ironically, place further pressure on the state to provide policy responses to address the needs of various interests. These interests may well often find themselves at odds with each other, further complicating policy development and implementation and contributing to a more dynamic and competitive policy-making process. The prerogatives and pressures exerted by foreign governments on Korean economic policy are also keen. For example, the Kim Young Sam administration announced in December 1994 a new initiative for internationalization (*segyehwa* in Korean) as the prime goal of the government. In 1996, Korea gained admission to the Organization for Economic Development and Cooperation (OECD). These economic developments and policy responses reflected, in part, a response to Western pressure to open markets and Korea's own need for greater penetration of foreign markets.

Economic liberalization created undesirable by-products for the authoritarian executive–bureaucratic nexus: primarily the differentiation and pluralization of middle-class interests. Different interest groups tried to represent their interests in the political arena but soon found political space closed. Interest groups with middle-class origins found out that, without opening the closed noncompetitive political system, their interests could not be realized in the political arena. The middle class thus refused to submit to the state-imposed authoritarian order and demanded more freedom. The entry of the middle class into the fray of social and political liberalization strengthened the hand of the democratic coalition and put it on equal footing with the ruling power bloc (see Han 1995, for details). As a result, the authoritarian executive–bureaucratic nexus faced mounting pressure from *chaebols* and labor, but also faced opposition from what heretofore had been a relatively quiescent middle class.

This transition was seriously challenged when the authoritarian executive–bureaucratic arrangement went through political and economic restructuring with democratic consolidation. Under the current civilian government of President Kim, the conventional techniques of press control, such as prior restraint and postpublication censorship, have disappeared to a great extent. President Kim has been decisive in pursuing anticorruption campaigns, political reforms, and demilitarization, as evidenced by purging politicized military circles. He also seems to have effectively dismantled the core power bloc of the so-called the "TK group," a well-entrenched cadre of elites from the Taegu-Kyungbuk province with close personal ties to previous presidents. He thus has been able to draw wide support, impressively broadening the social basis of his reform politics (Han 1995; M. Kang 1995). While these initiatives have garnered support, as time goes by the president's leadership may encounter difficulties. This was evident after the disappointing results of the 1995 local government elections, which called into question the credibility of Kim Young Sam's presidential leadership. Some of the original supporters who put him into power have been disillusioned by what they perceive as a slow pace of change. The Kim administration seems to be quite unable to accommodate popular forces into some kinds of reform policies. Tensions are already beginning to mount, as can be seen in turbulence involving agriculture, environment, labor, and other domestic policy issues (Han 1995).[8]

Institutional changes, brought on by social, economic, and political forces, have diminished the absolute influence of the president over the bureaucracy and the bureaucracy over other social and business actors and policy control. Presidents Park and Chun enjoyed all but absolute control over policy design and objectives through the authoritarian structure of the Korean presidency and bureaucracy and their nexus. While effective in setting the agenda, particularly for economic policy, such assertions of will did not necessarily bode well for Korean development, as various episodes during the tenure of the presidents illustrate (for details see Hahm and Plein 1995). Social change and democratization in Korea have changed the presidency, the bureaucracy, and their relationship.

Individual Motives: Risks and Opportunities in a New Korea

The transformation from authoritarian to democratic arrangements will alter the set of incentives, choices, preferences, and arrangements in which individual bureaucratic actors operate. In essence, the set of givens which has guided activity under authoritarian arrangements has been disturbed. Current conditions are essentially in a state of flux, lending an air of uncertainty. Forces of both social and institutional change have converged to alter the bureaucratic environment sharply. These conditions will pose a threat to a number of variables identified in traditional rational-choice arrangements. For example, Monroe (1991:78) determined that consistent and stable preference orderings, clear knowledge of self-interest, and adequate information foundations are fundamental to rational-choice action. By identifying some of the dynamics of change, we can begin to speculate about possible bureaucratic responses in an era of uncertain outcomes, limited information bases, and the breakdown of rigid hierarchical arrangements.

Throughout the developmental experience, Korean bureaucrats have enjoyed a great deal of power (for general discussions, see Jacobs 1985; P. Kim 1993). This power has stemmed primarily from the control of information and implementation resources necessary to create and execute policy effectively. The ability to collect, process, and disseminate a wide range of information about domestic and international conditions has been a key power of the Korean bureaucracy. Indeed, there is still great power and prestige associated with the bureaucracy. Traditionally, career bureaucrats were more directly influential in state policy and could resist policy pressure from elected legislators. In addition, ties based on familial and school relationships were important in sustaining bureaucratic homogeneity (see Jacobs 1985). In short, until recently, bureaucratic life in Korea could be characterized as one of stability, prestige, and, within the confines of policy implementation and advisory functions, one of some degree of discretion and influence (Evans 1995).

But the social, political, and economic changes sweeping Korea have altered conditions and introduced new variables into the decision calculus of bureaucrats. There are a number of critical factors that will influence future bureaucratic behavior. These can be described as: (1) the declining prestige of the bureaucracy, (2) the potential use of bureaucratic entities as venues for interest access to policy making, (3) the decline of the strong presidential system, (4) relatedly, the emergence of fractious cabinet politics, (5) the growing crisis of the relevancy of the state in economic development, and (6) increasing presidential dependence on bureaucratic actors to deal with complex policy issues (for discussion, see Hanbek Delphi Research Team 1995).

The decline of prestige of the bureaucracy is palpable in Korea and is a reflection of changing socioeconomic conditions. On one dimension, there is growing doubt among economic elites about the capacity of the state to maintain social stability and amenable economic conditions. Among the masses, there is increasingly fierce popular rejection of *kwanjon minbi* (the government's traditional primacy over the people). Whereas the former hold that the state's decline is attributable to its lack of efficacy in guiding economic activity, the latter see the state, and by extension bureaucrats, as a force that has in recent times imposed heavy-handed restrictions on the freedom of expression and has suppressed consumer desires. This change in attitude has undercut one of the most important incentives to choosing a career in the public service—respect and prestige (see Hanbek Delphi Research Team 1995).[9] Under these circumstances, the bureaucratic apparatus of the state becomes seen less as an instrument for the realization of national goals and more as an impediment to their realization, whether these goals be economic or social.

Economic growth has also diminished the financial incentives for entering public service. The perception that lucrative opportunities may be found in private enterprise have undercut the material incentives for the best and the brightest to choose a public service career. Growing wage gaps between the public and private sectors contribute to the loss of prestige associated with the bureaucracy. Without these benefits, the quality of civil servants may diminish. Job security may become the primary attraction for a career in the bureaucracy. Combined, these factors may serve to hinder the recruitment of those most able to deal with the challenges of policy formulation and implementation in an era of institutional transition (Evans 1995). In such circumstances a career in the bureaucracy may be seen as a second-best option. Indeed, a career in the bureaucracy may be replaced by temporary office holders whose priorities rest in landing a job in the private sector. If the quality of public service suffers, so too will that of the ability of the bureaucracy to administer policy and execute programs. Such diminished capacity will reinforce views that the state is superfluous. In turn, this will further lower the prestige and legitimacy of the bureaucracy (see Evans 1995; Hanbek Delphi Research Team 1995).

A second factor affecting bureaucratic arrangements deals with the influence that sectoral and organized interests will be able to exert on administrative arrangements. Absent an effective legislature, the bureaucracy will be seen as the primary venue for access to decision-making arrangements. Bureaucrats, hoping to maintain and build influence over policy matters, may seek to build constituencies and power bases by reaching out to organized interests. By the same measure, agencies may become susceptible to capture. With socioeconomic and political liberalization, the coalitions of interest have become much more complex. Conflicts of interest among different government agencies have become more intense as well. This opens up new possibilities for leading *chaebols* to play on these internal divisions and to exploit them for their own purposes. This will be expressed as bureaucratic actors and entities begin to represent sectoral and other interests in the policy process. As the experiences of other highly evolved bureaucratic states suggests, there is no shortage of access points for private interests seeking desired policy outcomes and arrangements in such a system.

That bureaucratic arrangements may evolve into policy subsystems suggests a third factor relating to the decline of a strong presidency. A number of factors have contributed to the weakening of the president. Perhaps the most tangible has been the establishment of term limits for the president. The prospects for this changing the bureaucratic–executive calculus cannot be over-looked. In the past, the tenure of a president was uncertain; the idea of a fixed term will alter bureaucratic perceptions of reward and loyalty. President Roh's tenure was fixed and short, and marked by a weak presidential management style.[10] President Kim's term is fixed, a new reality in Korean politics, and is more dependent on coalition building and brokering among competing interests. Both the time horizon of presidential leadership and its management style directly affect the executive–bureaucratic arrangement in the policy process. In short, we might expect to see a greater degree of bureaucratic independence exerted as a result.

Under presidents Park and Chun, there was a strong principal–agent relationship between the president and the bureaucracy. For these presidents, the executive–bureaucratic nexus was marked by presidential efforts to direct and strengthen the bureaucracy against the inevitable tides of democratization and policy com-plexity. Also, the bureaucrats could see the continuity of presiden-tial policy initiatives. This continuity created considerable stability in basic policy by permitting the bureaucracy on policy affairs to engage in long-term and consistent planning without fear of sudden or unexpected policy conflicts or shifts. Bureau-cratic loyalty to the president granted extensive administrative dis-cretion and provided a basis for job security and professional advancement. As a consequence, policy could succeed if mutual consent between the president and the cabinet ministers was accomplished. In this regard, there have been positive impacts of the bureaucracy on economic and industrial development.

However, coupled with political democratization and eco-nomic liberalization and globalization, new presidential arrange-ments will alter the playing field of bureaucratic–executive relations. For example, bureaucrats may tend to resist ambitious presidential initiatives for economic and industrial development. Sensitive to presidential politics, bureaucrats would likely see such initiatives as temporary. Championing one might damage the bureaucrat's fortunes under future presidents. As a result, those with long-term career ambitions may be hesitant to dedicate themselves to short-term presidential initiatives. In short, loyalty to the president may not guarantee positive career prospects. The impact of such caution and resistance may alter the relationship between the president and the bureaucracy and, by extension, the policy outcomes observed. The new liberalized conditions may also contribute to fragmentation and conflict over the boundaries of bureaucratic jurisdictions and funding. As a result, "turf wars" among cabinet ministries have rapidly increased.

Thus, not only does the prospect of fixed presidential terms alter the calculus of bureaucratic strategies and actions, but so also does the present nature of the presidential cabinet system. This constitutes the fourth factor that will influence bureaucratic choices and actions in the future. In the past, the strong president-centered system all but guaranteed that cabinet ministers would toe the presidential line. The cabinet served to amplify and clearly communicate presidential preferences to the bureaucracy. Due to changes in the Korean political arena, this is no longer the case. As Korea gropes to develop a party system that is based less on presidential personality and allegiance and more on broad ideo-logical and policy agendas, the composition of the presidential cabinet will change. In essence, there will be more diversity and instability in presidential cabinets; as a result, bureaucrats will likely get mixed signals from their executive principals, and presidential prerogatives might become distorted. This trend is clearly evident in contemporary Korean politics, where the ruling party has been cobbled together by combining elements of entrenched regime members and established opposition leaders. The fact that the long-standing opponent to the Chun and Roh regimes, Kim Young Sam, would come to be president under his predecessors' banner is evidence of the topsy-turvy climate of Korean politics.

This turmoil is reflected in executive arrangements. In efforts to accommodate the diverse coalitions which make up the ruling party, Korea has been wrestling with a quasiparliamentarian approach to government, albeit without the parliamentary base (Bedeski 1994:46). Elements of the ruling party coalition have sought to gain seats in the presidential cabinet, since this is where the action is. In short, the instability of the Korean party system is now being imposed upon the bureaucracy. In times of authoritar-ian control, the question of party stability is moot; in times of democratic transition it becomes paramount. The lack of atten-tion given to the relationship between party system stability and bureaucratic behavior is sorely lacking in the literature of both developing and developed countries.

The fifth factor influencing bureaucratic behavior is what might be termed an identity crisis vis-a-vis the role of the state in the economy. In short, there now exists a sense of crisis as to the relevance of the state in economic development and uncertainty as to what course future policy actions should take. Throughout the 1960s and the 1970s, organized business interests, primarily in the form of *chaebols*, were "junior partners" to the state (Im 1990:246). But policy actions and market forces changed the balance of this relationship dramatically through the 1980s and 1990s. Present conditions suggest that the influence of the state is slipping and that there is a growing perception that it is becoming more of a drag on the economy than a catalyst for development. Concessions made by the Chun regime to business interests, which primarily took the form of easing state controls over banking and finance, diminished the influence of the state. Furthermore, this time period saw the rapid expansion of *chaebol* influence over the market (see Amsden 1989:116). International and technological forces also conspired against the government; the applicability of foreign investment controls that had worked so well during the 1960s and 1970s lost its effectiveness in the 1980s and 1990s, due to the changing nature of technology which strengthened the hands of foreign originators of new products and production processes (see Hahm, Plein, and Florida 1994). We will return to, and expand upon, this theme in chapter 5.

Given conflicting interpretations and objectives regarding the role of the state, the executive–bureaucratic arrangement may no longer be able to speak with one voice. At the end of the 1980s, some of the strongest pressure for diminishing the state's intervention role came from precisely those elite agencies, like the Economic Planning Board (see Evans 1995). Bureaucrats in these agencies, often American-educated economists and thus far from being "statists," tended to embrace neoliberal policy prescriptions. They believed that minimizing the state's role was the best way to promote development.

In short, there is a growing perception that capital interests now should enjoy greater discretion in pursuing their own self-directed economic ends. Instead of depending on the state for sustenance and guidance, the perception of the state is increasingly that of an ally which will assist in smoothing market operations and reducing market uncertainty through such efforts as preferential regulatory arrangements and other protective devices, placating labor demands, and facilitating international trade. While some in the current government understand that the role of the state is shifting away from sectoral regulation and toward general market regulation (see Glain 1995), whether the bureaucratic structure as a whole can accept and negotiate this change is uncertain. In short, these conditions are likely to contribute to divisions between bureaucratic entities.

Sixth, apart from sociopolitical dimensions which have changed the bureaucratic–executive nexus, there has been the growing prominence of complex technical policy issues, problems, and responsibilities that the government is expected to address. One of the factors responsible for the transformation of the Korean presidency is the admission by recent presidents that policy formulation and implementation responsibilities need to be ceded to bureaucrats because of the technical complexities of policy issues relating to such areas as economic, industrial, and technological development (see Hahm and Plein 1995). Obviously, the devolution of policy formulation responsibilities increases opportunities for administrative influence and self-promotion, and with this the attendant interbureaucratic conflict and competition which is bound to arise. This change has helped to accelerate and deepen the transformation that social and economic liberalization fomented.

In summary, the critical variables that influence the actions and choices of bureaucratic actors are now in flux. Korean bureaucrats are faced with cross-cutting conditions. On one hand, the place of the bureaucracy in Korean society has been undermined by a loss of faith in its capabilities to provide guidance and direction in social and economic progress. Coupled with this is a factionalized party system which has served to divide presidential cabinets, leading to mixed policy signals that bureaucrats must decipher. Further, a fragmented bureaucracy makes individual agencies susceptible to capture from sectoral interests. On the other hand, in an age when the power of the presidency is declining, bureaucrats stand to gain in the balance of power between the two institutions. Since the presidency and the bureaucracy have been the two most viable institutions in Korea, this increase in power would be significant. Bureaucrats could stand to enjoy increased influence as conduits and shapers of sectoral interests and primary players in associated policy subgovernments or subsystems. Furthermore, bureaucrats can claim legitimacy for their ascent by emphasizing their role in policy making as necessitated by the growing technical complexity of policy problems, issues, and responsibilities.

CONCLUSION

Understanding the dynamics of state development is a daunting enterprise. Insights on the developmental experience can be gleaned from the synthesis and refinement of existing approaches. The framework developed here takes into account elements of the deterministic perspective outlined in modernization theory and other structuralist approaches that emphasize the influence that contextual factors have in shaping the evolution of political institutions and arrangements. The framework also utilizes elements of the rational-choice perspective, emphasizing that political and bureaucratic actors will act in what they take to be their own best interests, given prevailing conditions and their knowledge of rewards and consequences.

Through a perspective that combines elements of structural determinism and rational-choice approaches, we have been able to offer an assessment of the evolution of executive–bureaucratic arrangements in the Korean experience. By understanding structural factors we can identify how various cultural, historic, economic, social, and international factors have influenced the structure of institutional arrangements in the Korean state. Within these institutional arrangements, we have described from a rational-choice perspective how political and bureaucratic actors have changed patterns of behavior in order to adjust to transformations. We argue that our framework better helps to explain critical episodes in the Korean experience involving the state, especially its presidential and bureaucratic components. From our review of the Korean experience, we are able to offer the following observations.

First, in strong-authoritarian state arrangements, hierarchical arrangements are rigid and enforced by unsubtle power relations between executive leadership and the bureaucracy. In the Korean case, we can argue that authoritarian arrangements initially emerged from the convergence of a number of structural conditions—such as the threat of North Korea, postcolonialism, and the absence of established labor and capital actors. However, these arrangements were not structurally *determined*, but were influenced by the context which social, political, and economic conditions created. This aspect of contextual influence coupled with the independent choices made by political actors helps to explain why the Korean experience, and presumably other specific state experiences, do not fit comfortably into the broad framework of general deterministic models.

Second, because regime goals are rather immediate and because they are reactive to perceived threats and challenges from within state arrangements from such societal actors as capital and labor, authoritarian arrangements are inherently unstable. The often far-ranging policy imperatives of such regimes, such as the repression of labor and the acquiescence to capital demands during the Chun regime, converged to create new structural features which changed the conditions in which political and institutional strategies, decisions, and actions take place.

Third, it can be said that the Korean authoritarian state was a victim of the economic successes that it helped to facilitate (see Park 1991; Koo 1993b). Contrary to the interpretation of others (Haggard and Kaufman 1995; Amsden 1989), Korea has not yet successfully negotiated the transition to postauthoritarian arrangements. For example, Haggard and Kaufman (1995) argue that an economic crisis brings forth a crisis of legitimacy for that state, forcing change and transformation. They argue that the Korean state navigated its economic crisis by effectively designing successor arrangements that are more liberal and democratic. We argue that the transformation of the Korean state has been more accidental than purposeful. It is the outgrowth of short-term strategies employed by both the Chun and Roh regimes to remain in political control. In essence, in an effort to preserve its hold on authority over students and others striving for social liberalization, these regimes ironically transferred the reins of power to economic interests by divesting strong state controls over the marketplace. Fortunately for Korea, a well-established bureaucracy has been adept at making the most of this transition by helping to facilitate positive short-term economic outcomes in the post-Chun and Roh era. Nevertheless, questions regarding the viability of the bureaucracy in a rapidly transforming postauthoritarian state remain.

Fourth, in the Korean experience, postauthoritarianism has radically changed the expectations and strategies for political leadership and bureaucracy alike. Despite the overall decrease in the role of the state bureaucracy vis-a-vis the market, given an authoritarian tradition in Korean politics, even under social democratization and economic liberalization, the executive–bureaucratic nexus will likely remain the primary locus of continued progress in economic and industrial development. These factors pose both opportunities and challenges for Korea. The key element to respond to these pressures will rest in the ability of the executive–bureaucratic arrangement to capitalize on social, economic, and international changes. But for it to be successful in meeting domestic needs and facing the future, a more adaptive stance for the executive–bureaucratic nexus will need to be taken. Such a posture will likely involve an embrace of democratic social change as a primary component of policy development strategies. This stance will likely require the effective involvement of bureaucratic, political, industrial, and other social actors in both policy formation and execution.

Lastly, bureaucratic agents see their options as rather circumscribed under authoritarian arrangements. As authoritarian regimes mature and become a more stable presence in society, there emerges a greater dependence on bureaucratic apparatus. Given their familiarity and tenure, the influence of bureaucratic actors may be enhanced by becoming agents of institutional memory. In postauthoritarian arrangements, the bureaucracy may provide a stabilizing force and a source of continuity through presidential transitions and with the entry of new institutional actors, such as a more influential Korean legislature, into policy matters. In this sense, not only is the expertise of bureaucrats in technical matters appreciated, but their input on policy formulation and feasibility may also become more valued.

NOTES

1. This is not to say that the study of executive–bureaucratic relations in authoritarian states has not grown over the years. For example, Wade (1992) explored how strong authoritarian regimes have come to depend on bureaucratic arrangements while at the same time taking steps to exert absolute control over their functions. Kasza (1987) identified how

bureaucratic actors can be a force of policy innovation in authoritarian states, such as in the cases of Japan, Peru, and Egypt. Haggard and Kaufman (1995) traced the manner in which authoritarian states manage the transformation to more democratic arrangements. In their analysis, economic crisis brings forth a crisis of legitimacy for the state, forcing change and transformation. The study of the dynamics of authoritarian–bureaucratic relations can be seen in the context of a body of literature dealing with transformations and the effect of exogenous economic shocks on the stability of authoritarian, democratic, and other system arrangements. These studies tend to have a structuralist orientation which explores the effect of economic conditions on the legitimacy of existing governmental arrangements (see, for example, O'Donnell 1973; Gasiorowski 1995; Haggard and Kaufman 1995). This line of research, in itself, can be seen as an outgrowth of a well-established body of literature with roots in modernization theory. A flowering of research in this area is a likely response to the flurry of regime changes that have emerged in the developing world and Eastern Europe in recent years.

2. Kitschelt (1992) makes an important observation that it is difficult to separate the structuralist and rationalist approaches in practice since scholars tend to combine elements of both approaches when executing studies. In fact, he notes that the dualism in approaches might best be characterized as divided along lines of structural and process dimensions, where the former emphasize the influence of institutions (the state, class, economic structure) and the latter emphasize triggering events that have disturbed existing arrangements. Colclough (1991:7–11) makes a similar observation regarding the orthodoxy of the neoliberal position on defining free trade as a term or standard. He notes that discussions of the neoliberal position become clouded because a policy that might be considered free trade by one adherent to this perspective, might be defined as interventionist by another. The distinction of our approach is twofold. First, we seek to identify consciously the structural and rational elements of our approach. Second, we seek to concentrate on the effects of regime change on one key political institution, in this case the Korean presidency and bureaucracy.

3. In this regard, Im (1990:257) notes, "[Historically] the overdeveloped state in Korea—overdeveloped in repressive state apparatus—provides a clear advantage and great freedom of choice to the power bloc in charge." In other words, Korea already had in existence the institutional arrangements and resources necessary to initiate and exert bureaucratic authoritarianism. These arrangements were, in part, a holdover from the Japanese colonial experience (see Koo 1993b:234), as well as from the regime of Syngman Rhee, which lasted from 1948 to 1960.

4. Through policy actions taken in 1961, control of the financial industry came firmly under the hands of the government. By directing, and denying, credit and loans to various firms and sectors, the government had a superior relationship to capital interests (Steers, Shin, and Ungson 1989; E. Kim 1994). The government also laid claim to the distri-

bution of foreign aid, an economic development source critical during the early stages of industrialization (E. Kim 1994). Finally, the government exerted great control over the flow of foreign direct investment through restrictions and the use of technology-licensing arrangements (Mardon 1990; Hahm, Plein, and Florida 1994).

5. In late 1994 the EPB was reorganized into the Ministry of Finance and Economy, which was created by combining the EPB and the Ministry of Finance.

6. In fact, the Park regime restricted democratic reform severely through the Emergency Decree on National Security and the Yushin Constitution at the end of 1971 and 1972, respectively. In this regard, Im (1990) argues that a strengthened authoritarian regime was initiated through the emergency decree and that its establishment was completed with the Yushin Constitution.

7. For example, during the Park regime, the bureaucracy had to acquiesce to presidential demands to implement a program of investment in the heavy and chemical industries. Although elements of the bureaucracy warned that such an effort was economically unsound, given Korea's state of development, such warnings were pushed aside and the initiative was pursued (see Hahm and Plein 1995). Once adopted, the Korean bureaucracy was effective at carrying out the dictates of the mandate, though the economic consequences for the country were dear.

8. The recent history of Korean politics is quite complex. In early 1990, faced with growing opposition in the National Assembly, the Democratic Justice Party of President Roh Tae Woo merged with the two leading opposition parties. Among those brought into the party were Kim Young Sam, of the progressive Reunification Democratic Party, and Kim Jong Pil, representing the more conservative National Democratic Republican Party (Bedeski 1994:18;45). In late 1995, the prospects of party stability were called into question due to the arrests of former President Roh Tae Woo on bribery charges stemming from his tenure in office and former president Chun Doo Hwan for his role in the 1979 coup that brought him to power and the subsequent military crackdown on student protestors at Kwangju in 1980. President Kim Young Sam's role and response to these arrests reveal a political actor uncertain as to how to position himself in the midst of controversy. In April 1996, a narrow victory in the Korean congressional elections signaled that the credibility of the Kim administration had been preserved to some degree. Kim sought to distance himself from his predecessors, going to such lengths as to rename the political party which he heads prior to the election. In August 1996, both Chun and Roh were convicted of charges brought against them. Chun Doo Hwan was convicted of taking bribes and complicity in staging the overthrow of President Park in 1979 and violently suppressing student demonstrations in Kwangju in 1980. Roh Tae Woo was found guilty of taking bribes from major industrialists and supporting Chun's actions in 1979 and 1980. A number of high ranking government officials from the Chun and Roh administrations as well were convicted on similar counts. In

addition, a number of industrialists were also tried and convicted on bribery charges. In December of 1996, Chun, Roh, and others appealed their cases to the Korean Supreme Court. Prior to this appeal, these individuals were successful in gaining reduced sentences. Chun's sentence was changed from death to a life term in prison, while Roh's prison term was reduced. The convicted industrialists were given probation.

The bribery scandal was just one of a number of crises faced by the Kim administration in 1996 and 1997. Two policy initiatives led by the Kim administration were the source of considerable political and social discord. In December of 1996, the Kim administration pushed legislation through the National Assembly that revised laws dealing with internal security arrangements and organized labor. The laws were passed in a controversial meeting of the legislature where opposition parties were excluded from participation. The new security law was met with resistance by those who felt that too much power still remained in the hands of Korea's National Security Planning Agency (the former Korean Central Intelligence Agency). This institution has long been seen as a threat to civil liberties in Korea. In the same session, a controversial labor law was passed. Adopted ostensibly to satisfy expectations under Korea's membership in OECD, the law was seen as eroding guarantees for lifetime employment in firms. Particularly nettlesome to labor were provisions that delayed until the year 2000 formal recognition of numerous labor groups. Without such recognition, these groups are essentially illegal. The new labor law met with massive strikes on a scale unparalleled in Korean history. In the midst of this turmoil the Kim administration and the ruling New Korea Party suffered a loss of legitimacy as both domestic and international groups, including the OECD, criticized both the process by which the legislation had been passed and the substance therein. Responding to this criticism, the Kim administration reconsidered its hard-line stance against popular and labor demonstrations and engaged in efforts to resolve this crisis. The outcome of this debate remains to be seen. Kim's difficulties intensified with another bribery scandal in early 1997. In this controversy, it was discovered that high ranking public officials had received bribes from the Hanbo steel company in return for their putting pressure on banks to extend credit to the company. A son of Kim has been implicated in the scandal.

9. The Hanbek Delphi Research Team has conducted detailed empirical survey analysis of Korean bureaucrats' attitudes toward state political institutions.

10. A similar argument can be made that President Chun Doo Hwan's frequently expressed commitment to a single seven-year term eroded his ability to exert influence over the bureaucracy and business interests (see Cotton 1992).

4

Presidential Leadership and Technology Policy

In the Korean experience, presidential orientation toward policy strategy and planning has served as a barometer of state action. The lack of mature institutional balances and checks on the president has traditionally made his mandates absolute. Even the bureaucracy, often identified as a strong institutional presence, has been structurally dependent on, and vulnerable to, presidential prerogative. Until recently, presidential orientation toward technology policy has long held that technology is primarily a means of securing broader economic and industrial development goals, such as in export promotion and basic manufacturing. However, a combination of factors has contributed to subtle shifts in presidential influence over the past thirty years to give technology policy considerations higher priority. These factors are a combination of two trends. Appearing first was the trend toward increasing technological sophistication as a key component of economic development. The second trend, in large part, has been an outgrowth of economic development—namely, the erosion of strict authoritarian power in the face of economic liberalization and nascent democratization.

As the Korean economy has developed since the early 1960s, the need for greater sophistication in the development and application of technological processes has been clearly demonstrated. Primarily geared to establishing and maintaining market niches in the global economy, the move toward technological capacity has more recently reflected a need to satisfy increasing consumer demands at home as well. Each step in Korea's sequential strategy of moving from labor-intensive basic industries to more sophisticated capital-intensive production processes has emphasized increased capacity to absorb, apply, and in some instances to develop needed technologies. Given the current emphasis on such complex areas as electronics, biotechnology, telecommunications, and semiconductor memory products, a premium has been placed on technological capacity in recent economic planning and development efforts. In this regard, recent administrations have begun to entertain the notion that Korea can participate in technological innovation, rather than concentrate solely on the adoption of technologies to facilitate industrial activity.

The complexity of policy planning for technological innovation has vested greater influence in the hands of those in the bureaucracy with jurisdiction over matters relating to science and technology. Those within the higher circles of the office of the president are wrestling with the fact that economic planning will require the input of these bureaucratic echelons' interests. As we will detail, overcoming past practices which saw the president imposing his will over the bureaucracy may meet some difficulty. Compounding the ascendancy of administrative actors are the forces of political and economic liberalization. Political change has taken the form of democratization. This has been most clearly expressed in terms of an invigorated legislature and public opinion, which are beginning to gain access to policy discussion, if not policy decision.

As the coalitions of political interest become much more complex, conflicts of interest among different political actors, including different government agencies, become more intense. This in turn opens up new possibilities for sectoral interests to play on these divisions and to exploit them for their own purpose. As a result, presidential influence has been modified by the gradual decrease of absolute control over policy direction. This in itself is the product of the growing influence of bureaucratic and other political actors, popular demands for democratization, and external economic influences, such as natural resource shortages and world financial market adjustments, that lay outside the president's sphere of control. In short, whereas the president used to have absolute control over the policy process, he must increasingly act as a broker between often-conflicting interests among private and public actors.

The changing role of the presidency, the enduring importance of the bureaucracy in shaping and implementing policy, and the emergence of sectoral pressures are well-illustrated in the case of Korea's efforts to coordinate technological development. In this chapter, we will explore the role of the presidency in directing Korea's technological development. Such a review reveals a number of interesting themes that illustrated the transition of the developmental state into its postdevelopmental form. First, an analysis of Korea's strongest president, Park Chung Hee, illustrates the absolute control enjoyed by authoritarian regimes over the course of economic development-related technology policy. Park all but directed policy, sometimes to the chagrin of senior bureaucratic advisors. In the case of President Chun Doo Hwan, we see the power and influence of the authoritarian state begin to fray. In a desperate attempt to retain power, Chun sought to crush labor and student dissent and make accommodations to capital interests to shore up support. During this period of turmoil, Chun came to depend on close appointed allies in the Ministry of Science and Technology to advance his policy agenda. Under President Roh Tae Woo the winds of social and economic change began to be felt, reaching their full force under President Kim Young Sam. Under both these presidents the combination of a diminishing role of the state in determining technological development and industrialization outcomes, competing sectoral interests, and a competitive political arena changed the dynamics of presidential leadership. This is particularly true for President Kim Young Sam. For future presidents, we surmise that a premium will be placed on their ability to act as brokers among contending interests and crafters of the political coalitions necessary to achieve policy objectives.

PRESIDENTIAL PRIORITIES AND THE PLACE OF TECHNOLOGY POLICY[1]

President Park Chung Hee (1961–1979)

Current Korean economic policy strategy reflects the legacy of President Park Chung Hee. His two-decade tenure set the stage for subsequent governments. The strong imposition of "top-down" policy planning and implementation; the targeting of certain preferred industries and commercial entities; the reliance on personal, rather than institutional, arrangements as the engine of governance; and a linear approach to economic development that perceived industrial ability as a series of sequential steps moving to greater sophistication are all hallmarks of the Park regime.

Through a bloodless military coup, Park Chung Hee assumed power in May 1961. President Park quickly asserted firm control over various areas of domestic and foreign policy, including economic development. Concentrating on economic development policy schemes, President Park initiated the first of several successive five-year plans in 1962. In 1963 the plan was revised to emphasize export promotion (see Hahm 1994; Hahm, Plein, and Florida 1994). Strongly nationalistic and influenced by Japanese corporatist approaches, Park sought to mobilize economic development and enlist popular support under the rubric of a renaissance of the nation through the buildup of independent economy (see Ernst 1994; Korean Ministry of Science and Technology 1980). President Park saw his political survival as dependent on export-led economic growth; to achieve this he strengthened the hand of the economic technocrats under his political authority.

Park's eighteen-year tenure as chief executive reveals how success in achieving basic industrial capacity and the changing nature of technology needs and options shaped the contours of the administration's approach to these policy areas. As the years progressed, attention increasingly turned to technological development concerns. But throughout the Park administration, technology policy remained primarily an adjunct to larger export-oriented industrial development policy objectives. Because it was perceived in instrumental terms, technological development did not occupy a prominent place in the Park administration's primary vehicles for development—the Five Year Economic Plans (Y. Kim 1986).

The Park administration's orientation toward technological development embodied two phases. In the first, running from the early 1960s to the mid-1970s, technology policy was perceived primarily in instrumental terms. In the effort to transform an agrarian-based economy into one based on industry, technology was seen as a bridge to facilitate the development of primary industries. Emphasis was placed on encouraging the development of an infrastructure which would facilitate the adoption of technologies originating elsewhere. This was reflected in two primary policy goals at the time: manpower training to handle the new technologies and transfer-implementation strategies to apply the new technologies (Chin 1986; Choi 1986).

These policy goals took three forms. First, the Park administration initiated the development of physical infrastructure to encourage technological application. The establishment of the Seoul-Pusan Highway and later the initial construction of Daeduck Science Town (1970–1974) are two examples of this appreciation for physical infrastructure. Second, the Park administration encouraged the development of a scientific community through the establishment of various professional organizations and associations. Such efforts included the establishment of the Korean Science and Technology Center in 1962, followed by the establishment of the Korean Foundation of Science and Technology Societies in 1966, and the Korea Science Academy in 1976. Finally, the Park administration sought to put in place organizational structures to facilitate the role of technology in industrial development strategies. The most important of these were the Korea Institute of Science and Technology (KIST) and the Ministry of Science and Technology, established in 1966 and 1967, respectively. In short, Korea relied on the technology innovations of developed countries. The technology component of its industrial policy strategies focused on having the procedures and the skills in place in order to fully utilize these borrowed technologies. In the desire to seek short-term results, acquisition of foreign technology was preferred to strategies aimed at developing Korea's domestic technological capacity.

During this period, the primary bureaucratic players in the formation of these programs were the minister of the Economic Planning Board (EPB)[2] and the first senior presidential secretary for economic affairs. Another player in policy planning was the Ministry of Commerce and Industry (MCI).[3] As Park desired, the concentration of advisory power in the hands of the EPB allowed short-term policy initiatives aimed at immediate economic development results (e.g., export promotion) to prevail. Bureaucratic agencies more oriented toward long-term policy planning, such as the Ministry of Science and Technology (MOST), which pinned hopes on long-term technological development, primarily served in an advisory capacity.

The mid-1970s signified a shift in priorities and constituted the beginning of the second stage of Park's orientation to industrial policy. Realizing that a concentration in light, basic industries would not secure Korea's future, Park emphasized the development of heavy and chemical industries. This major shift of industrial policy toward the massive investment of heavy and chemical industries can be partially attributed to the security threat of North Korea and President Park's strong desire for a self-defense capability. Under this initiative, a number of large business groups were encouraged to establish modern plants through combinations of government-guaranteed loans in such sectors as petrochemicals, chemical steel, machine building, and, later, automobiles and electronics. The shift to a heavy industry policy marked new demands on the supporting role that technology policy arrangements were to play (Korean Ministry of Science and Technology 1986b).

To continue the success of exporting heavy and chemical products, the government encouraged firms to increase their efforts to assimilate the imported technologies. Aimed at increasing domestic capability to absorb imported technologies, three areas were targeted to help facilitate movement into these complex areas. First, calls were made for expanded capacity for government research and development. Second, institutions of higher learning were encouraged to emphasize technical training. Third, priority was given to technology-transfer strategies aimed at placing foreign technology in the hands of the private sector. However, policy measures were focused only on absorbing the imported technologies for immediate technological necessities in production of a few selective strategic industries. That is, there was no explicit recognition of the importance of the indigenous creation of technology. In this regard, the export-oriented industrial policy still dominated technology policy.

But this change in priorities would soon display the shortcomings of policy based on presidential prerogatives. The decision for massive investment in heavy and chemical industries was made by only the president and his economic advisors in the Blue House (Korea's Office of the President) and the MCI, without consultation with industries and other related ministries. These actions were taken over the objections of the Economic Planning Board. The Blue House had not yet established channels of communication with industry and other experts to gather information, formulate industrial policies, and implement decisions, depending instead on a highly insular circle of presidential advisors. This is not to say that there were no close relationships between the president and a small number of *chaebols*, but the Korean case does not fit well into corporatist explanations of the role of the state in economic policy and planning. Therefore, a short-term policy failure resulted due to the lack of information, understanding, and expertise regarding the new direction of industrial policy necessary to formulate and implement policy effectively. As a result, the massive investment on these designated priority industries of the 1970s led to temporary excess capacity in these industries. Pursued because they were held to be key to export-oriented economic development, these massive investments in heavy and chemical industries turned out to be the main causes of a structurally unbalanced economy (H. Lee 1993).

The energy crisis during the 1970s precipitated a deceleration in the growth of the Korean economy that lasted throughout the rest of the decade. The timing of the crisis could not have been worse, happening as it did in the midst of industrial restructuring around petrochemicals and heavy industries. In addition to higher petroleum costs, the industries were burdened with higher interest rates on foreign loans. Domestic inflation ensued, but the drive for heavy industry could not be arrested. To make the situation worse, a major political crisis was precipitated by the assassination of President Park in late 1979. The situation was aggravated by a second oil shock sparked by the Iranian crisis of 1979. This combination of a sudden political vacuum with an extreme external economic shock only added to Korea's troubles. Many heavy industries laden with large foreign debt saw the maturity of their loans arriving with higher interest charges before substantial production began. A number of foreign investors in special export zones sought to move into other countries; many businesses were losing export markets; labor problems were mounting; some plants were being closed; and mass unemployment threatened (for further discussion, see H. Lee 1993; Koo 1993a; E. Kim 1994).

President Chun Doo Hwan (1980–1987)

At this critical moment, President Chun Doo Hwan came to office through a military coup. He explored ways to reinforce his political legitimacy through gaining stable economic growth and efficiency by means of reorganizing the industrial and technological infrastructure. The goal of industrial policy was set as "building a new image for Korea as a technologically advanced nation through improving industrial technology and strengthening international competitiveness" (Korean Ministry of Science and Technology 1981). The first half of Chun's tenure generally focused on industrial reorganization through state-led mergers and liquidations of inefficient firms to modify the then-existing investment plan for the heavy and chemical industry on a large scale to correct the misallocation of resources. For example, four existing companies in the power-generating equipment industry were merged into Korea Heavy Industries and Construction Co. Reflecting a preference for strong presidential control, Chun's policy strategy for rectifying the immediate crisis and planning for the future centered on the concentration and streamlined coordination of industrial and related technological activities, both in the private and public sectors.

In the name of efficiency, President Chun reorganized the administrative system particularly for major government-supported research institutes (GSRIs) under the supervision of MOST. The first senior presidential secretary for economic affairs, Kim Jaeik, was confident that increased technological capacity would be critical to the second takeoff of national economic development. This belief was echoed by his successors. Kim Jaeik understood the existing problems of the operation of the GSRIs as primarily organizational. In his view, the fact that GSRIs operated separately under five different ministries without any centralized coordination spelled inefficiency. As a result, both Kim Jaeik and the Minister of MOST recommended that GSRIs be brought under the direct supervision of MOST (see Chun 1982; Hyun 1986; Korea Advanced Institute of Science and Technology 1986). Accepting this advice, President Chun recognized that the strength of consolidation rested on coordination and cost savings.[4] With the adoption of the plan in 1981, the GSRIs were brought under the aegis of MOST and their number was reduced from sixteen to eight through mergers (Ahn 1989).

In order to give direction to GSRI activity, MOST carried out the National R&D Project for the efficient use of direct government large-scale research funding. This action was fully backed by President Chun, who expressed his policy preferences through the National Congress for the Advancement of Technology (see Korean

Ministry of Science and Technology [MOST] 1982; 1985; 1987). Chaired by Chun, this body established the basic direction of the science and technology policy. This arrangement symbolized a shift in economic and industrial development strategy, reflecting a transition from export promotion to technological development. Efforts to give further direction to R&D through the GSRI mechanisms were amplified by increasing government commitment to funding support. Government spending grew substantially through the 1980s; so too did private R&D investment, eventually overtaking government support by a wide margin by the decade's end (Kim and Dahlman 1992). This trend serves as a reminder of the decreasing influence of the Korean government over economic activity as a result of rapid development.

In a sense, the Chun presidency provided a high-water mark for MOST, because the president clearly embraced the link of increased indigenous technology capacity to industrial development. Chun's interest was probably reinforced by the appointment of two of his long-time friends to the post of minister of MOST. This support allowed MOST to pursue policy preferences in the face of objection and criticism from bureaucratic representatives of other economic and industrial interests. But the changes of fortune for those championing technology development were driven by the forces of personality, reflecting the meeting of the minds of the president and his closest advisors. The glue that held together this arrangement was based not so much on institutionalized change as on personal relationships. Technology policies were made by only a few in MOST and the Blue House. These decisions were made without consultation with individual GSRIs and other related ministries and industries, and they sowed the seeds of policy failure. In essence, the Chun administration decided to shift emphasis to technological development and embark on a new economic development strategy without meaningful consultation with existing administrative actors with jurisdiction over such issues.

MOST failed to institutionalize channels of communication with other ministries, industry, and other related research institutes for policy recommendations. With the strong support of the president, MOST did not feel compelled to solicit the cooperation of industry, research institutes, and other ministries. What was agreed upon as policy could not be effectively implemented without clear paths of information, understanding, participation, and cooperation from various GSRIs, other industrial ministries, and individual industries. Those opposed to the concentration of technology policy control, such as the MCI, sought to challenge this new initiative.

The late 1980s should have been a time to consolidate and strengthen national technological capacity. The so-called "three low tides" (low interest rates, low oil prices, and the low value of the dollar) were extremely favorable to Korea. During this time, Korea made a significant recovery in economic growth. However, as a result of scandals in the financial institutions and his family, President Chun lost his public credibility and political legitimacy and thereby could do little to further technology development (Chung 1993).

President Roh Tae Woo (1988–1992)

President Roh Tae Woo, the handpicked successor of President Chun, had little time for technology policy. Concerned about the process of democratization and foreign policy with China, Russia, and North Korea, President Roh delegated broad authority on economic and industrial policy to his economic advisors at the Blue House, the minister of EPB, and other related ministries. With generally good macroeconomic conditions, the administration had little incentive to propose and change strategies for technology development. As a result, technology development planning received low priority in subsequent economic development planning.

But Roh would soon face important challenges that called for reconsideration of the place of technology in broader economic and industrial policy planning. At home, the pressure for greater democratization coupled with rising consumer demands gave life and voice to a nascent dissident labor movement. In the international arena, the advent of new, knowledge-intensive technology altered technology-transfer patterns. Foreign governments and private competitors, fearing the rapid assimilation of new technologies by developing countries such as Korea, were reluctant to license and share technologies, preferring instead to make direct investments and inroads into the markets of developing countries.

In this new environment, President Roh realized the importance of indigenous technological development, particularly the creation of new technology, for international competitiveness. He proposed, with his strong personal involvement, many policies for increasing competitiveness, particularly for the manufacturing industry. To increase competitiveness, the president and his first senior secretary for economic affairs, Moon Heegap, and later Kim Jongin, promoted increased specialization among big firms. His administration sought to encourage the top thirty firms to choose three core lines of activity to mitigate the increasing concentration of economic monopoly power and to increase investments in technological development.

The Roh administration expressed particular interest in the development of sophisticated technology as a means of meeting changes in the structure of international market arrangements. By the late 1980s, government officials were framing Korea's position in the world marketplace as being squeezed between newly industrializing states with lower wage rates and more advanced states which were at the forefront of capital-intensive knowledge industries, such as microcomputers and biotechnology. In response, the Roh administration championed the development of new export-oriented initiatives aimed at securing Korea's position in the international market. Examples of these included support for innovations in automotive technology and semiconductor memory products, both seen as key components for competition in the international marketplace.

In short, the Roh administration recognized that technology was no longer merely a means to industrialization, but had become a primary policy concern. In a rapidly changing international marketplace, a premium was placed on domestic indigenous technological capacity. Increasingly, the perception came to be that sophisticated technological ability subsumed industrial activity to a subordinate role as this newfound capacity provided the opportunity for greater flexibility, adaptability, and maneuverability in the international arena. But for Roh, it was too late to implement new policies because of his relatively weak political status, given a final-year term of office and his strong political involvement in the process of his succession.

President Kim Young Sam (1993–Present)

After a generation of military rule, a civilian regime was restored in 1993. The new government, headed by President Kim Young

Sam, inherits an economy in need of revitalization and facing the challenge of assessing whether the strong, president-centered strategies for economic development of the past should be used as a model for moving toward the future. With a stronger trend toward international protectionism on advanced technologies, President Kim and his first senior secretary for economic affairs appear to realize that the nature of future economic growth has become more dependent on the development of new technologies (*Hankuk Ilbo* 1993:12).[5] With this in mind, the administration is emphasizing the following science and technology activities to enhance domestic indigenous technology capability: (1) promoting private-sector R&D capabilities for high technology; (2) developing and acquiring high-caliber technological manpower; (3) localizing key strategic technology; and (4) expanding information and technology-intensive industries (Korean Ministry of Science and Technology [MOST] 1993).

Kim has made explicit his understanding of the close link between technological and economic development based on participation in the global marketplace. For example, in his New Year's message for 1994, Kim identified science and technology development as a keystone for the current five-year economic plan, noting, "We cannot enhance the international competitiveness of the Korean economy without greater technological development." Among the technologies specified in his speech were biotechnology, information processing, and research into new materials (see Y. S. Kim 1994; Glain 1995).

Technology advancement has become more critical because of poor recent macroeconomic performance (e.g., decrease in exports, particularly in the semiconductor industry) and a growing trade deficit. A component of the Kim administration's recent emphasis on technology development has been an easing of restrictions relating to foreign direct investment. Korea has long controlled forms of foreign investment through policy instruments aimed at controlling investment and licensing arrangements (see Hahm, Plein, and Florida 1994). By relaxing restrictions on foreign direct investment, Korea is seeking to attract technologically sophisticated production operations. The alternative to such a strategy is to require licensing arrangements between foreign corporations and Korean firms. However, holders of technological skills and processes are reluctant to divulge such prized capacities through joint arrangements.

President Kim Young Sam faces a difficult task in guiding technology policy development in a time of institutional change and rapid technological advance. From an institutional standpoint, the president will need to devote considerable efforts to effectively managing and coordinating the activities of various agencies (for a discussion, see Hahm 1994). This will be challenging for two reasons. First, the bureaucracy will likely enjoy greater influence over the policy-making process because of the complex and technical matters involved. Second, cooperation among the agencies is not assured. Clashing agendas, priorities, and outlooks on the appropriate course of technological development may well be at the heart of interagency conflict.

These managerial questions will be made more difficult by the changing nature of technology. Recent advances in applied science have made for dramatic developments in manufacturing processes involving biotechnology, telecommunications, electronics, computer technology, and other high-tech areas. Traditionally, the distinction between basic and applied research has been fairly well-defined. In such circumstances, policies could be crafted to enhance research or acquire technologies, depending on the dictates of needs and priorities. Today, the distinctions between research and development have become blurred. The immediacy of basic research to applications creates new market conditions and opportunities which make it difficult for government to effectively track and guide the path and pace of technological development. In addition, the specter of technological application can be the source of criticism by those fearful of negative consequences associated with new products and processes.

PRESIDENTIAL LEADERSHIP IN THE POSTDEVELOPMENTAL ERA

Through an historical overview, we have illustrated the evolution of Korean presidential orientations toward technology-based economic development strategies. The brief summary has revealed that a higher degree of technological sophistication had been sought after from administration to administration, to the point today where the ability to develop and apply new technologies stands on its own as a desirable outcome for economic planning. This transition from borrowing established technologies to engage in light industry to the targeting of the development of new technologies has not been smooth nor seamless. We have argued that presidentially imposed planning has not always met with success. So, too, we have noted how external shocks have derailed development plans. The conditions that contemporary Korean presidents face in directing policy initiatives relating to technology policy are much more complex today than in the past. It is enough that the technological sophistication required for new manufacturing and production activities places a premium on expertise and knowledge that may not exist within the president's inner circle. But added to this are the dynamics that economic and political liberalization has added to the policy mix.

One force of change is reflected in the movement toward the democratization of Korean politics and political institutions. In the past, a strong military state apparatus gave scant respect to organized opposition and popular dissent. Current President Kim Young Sam exercises his authority based on popular legitimacy. This means that possible sources of opposition and criticism will be allowed to participate to some degree in the policy formulation and review process. Two key actors in this regard are political parties and the legislature.

Political parties in Korea have traditionally been personality-driven and ephemeral. Tied to a single leader, parties existed for the sole purpose of victory; defeated, opposition parties had little standing in the all-or-nothing climate of Korean politics. Today, with the coming of democratization, there exists the real possibility that parties will become established fixtures in the political scene and broaden their base of organization beyond specific individuals and toward general policy preferences. If this maturation does occur, we can surmise that technologically oriented issues will become one component of party agenda. This is likely to be the case if Korea follows a path of development which provides for the emergence of a relatively well-educated and prosperous populace.

Historically, the dominance of authoritarian state–political and administrative arrangements has given considerable power to a bureaucracy and has created a stable cadre of professional politicians in the legislature as well. In fact, more than a few legislators begin their careers within the bureaucracy before seeking elective office. Thus, the expertise, power, and influence that are gained from government may have accrued to the political party and the legislature as well as to the bureaucracy. With the democratic reforms now at work in Korea, we can no longer disregard the independent impact of the legislature and the political party as a potentially important source of influence on technological development.

In the past, public opinion rarely seized on technological innovation as a critical issue. Like other societies in early stages of industrialization, the emphasis was on the ability to raise standards of living through transformation from an agrarian status. The public consciousness so often associated with postmaterialist and postindustrial societies is only now beginning to emerge in Korea (see Abramson and Inglehart 1995). Technology innovation is beginning to receive sporadic public attention in the popular press. This attention usually concentrates on the perceived risks and negative consequences of technological progress. A good example of this is the recent concern over nuclear energy and its waste disposal. Public concern over quality of life issues have found a voice through the mass media and will likely be expressed in the future through the interest group arrangements and through champions in the legislature and perhaps the bureaucracy.

The combination of party development and nascent public attention toward issues relating to technology means that Korean political institutions may have to change their ways. This will likely be most pronounced in the National Assembly, where heretofore technology has long taken a back seat to other economic development concerns (see Yoo 1988). For instance, in the legislature there has been no standing committee on science and technology affairs. In 1973, the legislature established the Economic and Science Committee, but this committee dealt primarily with macroeconomic affairs associated with the EPB. For political saliency, individual committee members have long held a similar view. As technology policy increasingly becomes a fixture in Korean policy planning, the legislature is taking steps to institutionalize science and technology policy planning and oversight arrangements. For instance, in 1994 the Korean legislature established a committee on telecommunications, science, and technology.

Political democratization is also closely tied with economic liberalization. Since the 1980s, the government has increasingly surrendered control over the business sector. This has taken a number of forms, ranging from the state's divestiture of bank holdings to relaxation of foreign direct investments, as well as relinquishing other instruments of credit control. This has had profound effects on the ability of the state to influence the course of economic development in general; it has also reoriented the relationship between the state and capital. Capital interests are increasingly at liberty to pursue economic activities of their own design. The size and dominance of *chaebols* means that much of the influence over economic development in Korea is shifting to the private sector.

Given the authoritarian Korean culture and political arrangements, the presidency will likely remain the primary locus of policy agenda-setting and initiation for technology innovation. But the forces of technological sophistication and the liberalization of politics and economy have eroded the absolute power once enjoyed by the president and the state over society, economy, and other political institutions. As a result, the president may increasingly find himself being a broker among contending interests. A premium may be placed on his skills to organize and sustain coalitions of sectoral and societal interests as a means of establishing and implementing economic development strategies.

In light of recent international market developments, socioeconomic democratization, and technological trends, as industrial policy comes to new high technological innovation, chances increase for fragmentation and conflict over the boundaries of bureaucratic jurisdictions and funding, causing "turf wars" among coalitions of other industrial ministries, politicians, and interest groups. These circumstances can lead to a lack of control and review of actual technology policy implementation (Presidential Council on Science and Technology 1991).

The demands of contemporary economic development planning suggest that in order to be effective, those ministries primarily engaged in technology policy implementation must be brought "on board" in policy planning, coordination, and review. In the Korean case, this means enlisting the cooperation and participation of the Ministry of Science and Technology (MOST) and the Ministry of Trade and Industry (MTI). In essence, this demands that cooperation be forged between two agencies with distinct but interrelated missions. This may be difficult, given the long contentious relationship between the research-driven MOST and the applications-driven MTI.

In the administrative system for technology innovation, MOST is responsible for coordinating technological research and development activities. But due to the relatively weak position of technology policy in industrial development schemes, the influence of MOST has been limited at best. In the past it has been the industrial ministries, such as the EPB and the MCI, which have been most influential in presidential policy planning for technological development. In particular, MOST has lacked influence over the direction and volume of research and development funding. In this subordinate situation, MOST has generally focused more on industry-related technology development than on the development of basic science. Moreover, ameliorating ministerial conflicts between MOST and MTI on science and technology activities will be challenging. For one thing, MTI may find this a threat, especially given the aggravated state of affairs that has existed since 1981 when supervision of GSRIs was transferred to MOST. MTI will be particularly sensitive to research initiatives which promise immediate application. Therefore, the establishment of primary technology policy planning and coordination responsibility across ministerial conflicts of interest in the office of the president and his cabinet may be necessary.

Under the strong-president system, the office of the president is structurally most able to influence policy coordination and implementation among related industrial ministries (Presidential Council on Science and Technology 1991). As discussed earlier, because technology has long been seen as a part of industrial policy, there have been periodic attempts to coordinate research and development efforts through presidential initiatives. In the early 1970s, the importance of the link between technology and industrialization in export-oriented development strategies emerged as a presidential priority. But these efforts were often tentative and limited to executive pronouncements of the importance of technology and the need for general cooperation to achieve development goals. Examples included the various conferences sponsored by the presidential administrations that were aimed at symbolizing a commitment to coordination and cooperation in science and technology-related policy activities—such as the Comprehensive Review Committee for Science and Technology, established in 1972, and the National Science and Technology Conferences, launched in 1982.

The first substantive steps toward institutionalized policy-planning coordination were made in 1991. The Presidential Council on Science and Technology (PCST) was established as the supreme advisory council for the president concerning science and technology policy in Korea, giving the science and engineering communities perhaps the highest-level access to the president. PCST is composed of eleven experts, including the minister of MOST as an *ex officio* member, and members appointed by the president for two-year terms. The council meets once every other week. Results of the meeting are reported to the president once a month by the chairman. There are several subcommittees, composed of select members of the main council, that carry out studies requested by the main council. The activities of these subcommittees are supported by twenty-five secretariats, who are on assignment from eight relevant ministries and six GSRIs. To date, the PCST has advised the president on such matters as "the basic policy for mobilization and allocation of science and technology investment resources" and "national policy for promotion of national competitiveness in the era of science and technology."

However, such advice has not strongly influenced presidential decision making and has not been reflected in policy implementation. These problems stem from the weak status of the PCST, which lacks strong legal and budget authority. In short, consistent, coherent, and feasible advice to the president and amelioration of ministerial conflicts on science and technology activities will likely require the strengthening and institutionalizing of a direct advisory system for science and technology affairs in the office of the president.

Throughout the Korean experience, an emphasis has been placed on administrative and policy coordination as a means of enhancing Korea's competitive position in the global economy. Following a trend toward concentrating advisory functions in the executive, the position of first senior presidential secretary for policy and planning was established in December 1994. A similar post was also established in the office of the prime minister.

Given the complexity of these responsibilities, the positions would seem to require individuals well-grounded in macroeconomic policy and sensitive to the role that technology plays in economic development. But such coordination will be challenging. The new realities of technological research and development center on the fact that there is often no fine line between basic research and application. As technology policy comes to new high technologies, as we noted earlier, chances increase for fragmentation and conflict over the boundaries of bureaucratic jurisdictions and funding. By giving a high priority to administrative coordination and policy implementation, the office of the president can help prevent such conflicts from breaking out.[6]

TECHNOLOGY POLICY IN THE POSTDEVELOPMENTAL STATE

Although the complexities of economic planning in an era of technological and democratic change have weakened presidential autonomy over policy control and direction, presidential influence will still be a force with which to be reckoned in Korea. Given the recent evolution of social, political, and administrative arrangements, we suggest that the influence and relative success of the president will be in large part a measure of his skills as a broker among contending bureaucratic, sectoral, and social interests. In order to achieve successful policy coordination, we would do well to draw on the lessons of the past. Two clear lessons emerge from revisiting past presidential initiatives. First, top-down imposition of policy priorities does not guarantee success. The experience of President Park reveals how personal preferences can be blind to external factors, in his case foreseeable factors in the international scene. Second, presidential policy preferences will not translate into lasting policy implementation without some degree of institutionalization. The technology development initiatives of the Chun administration illustrate how plans can be thwarted due to a lack of institutional development and sensitivity to established bureaucratic actors.

A third lesson emerges as well, but it is less clear. In the past, Korean presidents were able to operate independently of other political institutions. In the absence of developed countervailing political institutions, the president had free rein. But in a rapidly changing society where democratization is embraced, this is no longer the case. Conditions are changing, and while the president will remain the central force in policy affairs, consideration needs to be given to the inclusion of other policy actors in the process.

Given recent developments, the most immediate influence on economic and technological policy planning will likely be the bureaucracy. Current conditions suggest a paradox with which presidents will have to wrestle. Increasingly, the technological complexities of economic development planning will dictate an increasing voice for bureaucratic interests, at least in an advisory capacity. Ideally, this calls for insulating bureaucratic actors from both external and internal political pressures in order to encourage honest counsel on policy alternatives and recommendations. Thus, the president will become more dependent on these actors. Yet this is happening at the very time when bureaucratic actors are beginning to enjoy greater autonomy due to recently adopted presidential term limits, creating a condition in which bureaucratic actors may increasingly turn to sectoral constituencies as a source of support. In such an environment, different bureaucratic entities may become conduits for preferred policy options as mutually agreed to by their sectoral allies. This offers the specter of bureaucratic conflict on a scale that would make past disputes seem minor. Such circumstances could well be exacerbated if the Korean legislature fails to develop as a viable institution for channelling sectoral and organized interests.

In addition to these institutional factors, presidential policy coordination is also complicated by changing social and economic conditions. The current administration must face changes in the relationship between the state and the private sector. In the 1960s, the state could dictate economic development strategies because the nation's corporate base had yet to be developed. The absence of established players, entrenched interests, and organized peak associations allowed the government wide latitude. As the Korean economy has grown and its industries have become strong, the power of the state has diminished. Big firms have achieved greater autonomy and can block government measures that they perceive as against their interests. The state no longer controls meaningful financial resources in comparison to what is needed by industry; it no longer has the basic legal authority over many aspects of industrial policy that it once enjoyed in the past. This fact is especially relevant given the declining position of the

Korean government in controlling the extension of credit to private industry.

Furthermore, the voice of public opinion, as modulated by the press and organized interests, has greater resonance in Korean politics. Thus, for example, science and technology issues now must be considered within an increasingly influential social context. Democratization has given voice to risk consciousness over such issues as nuclear energy and its waste disposal. Public concern and the potential for popular resistance toward technology and science become variables that elected officials must keep in mind. While the executive has long enjoyed influence over industrial policy making, the legislature has merely ratified the decisions of the government, and criticism from opposition parties was muted. Today there is the distinct possibility that the legislature and political parties will evolve into players with whom to reckon.

Therefore, planning and coordination of technology policy will need to take into account factors that are making Korea a society in transition—namely, the twin forces of democratization and technological development. Given these forces of change and the legacy of past institutional arrangements, primary policy planning and coordination for technological development will likely be in the office of the president. Such an arrangement might include enlisting the support of government agencies engaged in technology research, development, and application, as well as allowances for more inclusive policy input by broadening the scope of participation in policy advice.

Through new institutional arrangements, authority for technology policy planning, implementation, and coordination might well rest squarely in the hands of the president. Unlike the past, when the power was directed from the top down, these new institutional arrangements would allow for advisory input from those with expertise in technology-related areas, as well as input of those sectors and interests that stand to be most affected by technological development. Such possibilities pose complex challenges for policy coordination and leadership. These conditions may well place a premium on presidential brokering skills. Such a development would be a significant departure from past presidential practices and would constitute an important change in the nature of the Korean presidency.

CONCLUSION

The complexities of the Korean developmental experience, be they in the rapid changes that have been made in the face of changing socioeconomic and technological factors or the internal dynamics of presidential–bureaucratic relationships, have proven elusive to those seeking to apply either the developmental state or neoclassical theory to explain state behavior. Judging from the literature, we surmise that this has likely been the case for efforts to explain other states as well. Our findings reinforce the need to develop more theoretical models that are more sensitive both to the forces of socioeconomic and technological transition and to the internal dynamics of institutional arrangements within the state. Our research suggests that there is a complicated linkage between the ability of the state to determine policy outcomes and the influence of exogenous social, technical, and economic factors in influencing policy planning and altering policy implementation once it is under way.

By using the case of Korean economic and technological policy planning and direction, we have sought to shed light on the transformation of the Korean presidency in an age of technological and social change. We have focused on what has been the preeminent political institution in Korea and have traced and charted developments which reflect the transformation of the Korean state. We have sought to describe how the state can respond to undifferentiated conditions, select a few areas for response, and embark on a path to help create the environment in which it will exist. Limits to such influence are imposed by both external conditions, such as developments in the global marketplace and changes in technology, and internal conditions, such as institutional politics and the consequences of policy outcomes—in the case of Korea, social and economic liberalization.

This chapter illustrates how, once policy initiatives are set in motion, the state will be forced to respond to intended and unintended consequences. This is clearly displayed in the Korean presidential attitudes toward the technological aspects of general economic planning and development. Once seen as an adjunct to policy planning, viewed merely as ends to facilitate the capacity to borrow manufacturing processes from developed countries, technological capacity and development is now seen as the centerpiece of Korean economic planning. None of this would have been possible had not initial industrialization schemes and export-oriented development strategies been implemented three decades ago.

Thus, a combination of external and internal forces has changed the face of Korean economic policy planning. Among the most fundamental of these changes may well be the nature of the Korean presidency itself. Throughout Korea's economic modernization, the presidency has set the direction, priorities, and objectives of economic development. As we have seen, past presidents imposed their will on the development process by relying on an inner circle of advisors to help lay out and execute policy strategies. Both the priorities and processes of policy intent were personality-driven. Such arrangements were a reflection of a president seeking to convert his vision into reality. Today developmental priorities are no longer the exclusive domain of the presidency, and the complexities of establishing a process for policy planning and coordination are far beyond a single actor's control. Instead, a new set of conditions exist which will likely emphasize the role of the president as a broker among contending policy recommendations and political interests.

Given present institutional realities, the Korean presidency will have to take a leading role in coordinating technology policy formulation and implementation. This role becomes more critical in an era of democratization, which sees the role of the president changing from one of absolute power to one that is more accommodating of divergent and sometimes competing interests. The president is uniquely positioned to set national policy priorities for technology innovation and for involving key government agencies to achieve policy aims. As we have argued in this chapter, such a new role for the president, both in the process of brokering and coordinating and in the substance of technology policy, will require new institutional arrangements aimed at providing the necessary venues and expertise for the development and implementation of technology-oriented policy. But for this desire to be transferred into reality, new institutional arrangements will have to be established to coordinate technology policy planning and implementation. Given the nature of Korean political and policy-making arrangements, such initiatives will need to concentrate on the office of the president.

NOTES

1. Much of the remainder of this chapter draws heavily on Hahm and Plein (1995).

2. As we noted earlier, in late 1994 the EPB was reorganized into the Ministry of Finance and Economy (MFE), which was created by combining the EPB and the Ministry of Finance.

3. The MCI was the forerunner of today's Ministry of Trade and Industry (MTI) and its earlier incarnation as the Ministry of Trade, Industry, and Energy (MTIE).

4. Under this plan, costly research facilities could be shared by personnel in various GSRIs, research programs could be coordinated, information and knowledge could be shared, and a healthy sense of competition could be instilled among the GSRIs. Consolidation also provided the opportunity for cost savings by restricting duplicative research and development efforts.

5. For example, the total amount of the budget for science and technology activities across administrations for fiscal 1994 was 1.96 trillion won. This represents a 33 percent increase over the fiscal 1993 budget of 1.48 trillion won. This increase is notable, compared to the annual average growth rate for science and technology activities, which has been 17 percent. In addition, the Kim administration established a "Biotech 2000" plan for promoting the bioengineering industry. The plan will be supported by 16 trillion won for ten major research projects across seven industry-related ministries by the year 2007.

6. Establishing primary technology policy planning responsibility in the office of the president might serve to better coordinate the general technological capacity-building activities expected of the state in market economies. The movement away from policy intervention in economic affairs and the ascendancy of capital interests does not mean that the role of the state in technology policy will evaporate. Indeed, we should expect sectoral interests to lobby for government programs that assist in technological research, development, and application. Such pressures will only further the need for the president to act in a brokering and coordinative capacity. Given the current climate of social and political change, coupled with the need for greater expertise in technology policy decision making, the process will need to be more inclusive of key advisory personnel who can help guide presidential decisions on technology policy. In this regard, we specifically outline a proposal for future institutional arrangements for Korean technology innovation policy planning and coordination (see Hahm 1994 for details).

First, the office of "first senior presidential secretary for science and technology" should be established to deal with science and technology affairs, with real authority to coordinate functions across ministerial conflicts of interests. Second, the first senior presidential secretary for science and technology should oversee the revitalized PCST as chairman. Members of PCST should include first senior presidential secretary for economic affairs and ministers and representatives of industry-related ministries. Under these arrangements, both technology policy and coordinated policy planning and formulation would be given a level of priority not seen before in the Korean experience. Third, the PCST and the first senior presidential secretary for science and technology would wield budget authority for science and technology activities. Without budgeting authority, initiatives of the PCST and the first senior presidential secretary for science and technology would have a limited chance of success. There is precedent for such arrangements, for the EPB (now MFE) enjoyed both authorization and appropriations powers in earlier economic development initiatives. The underlying idea is that planning divorced from budgeting might be purely symbolic, while budgeting without planning could lead to the misdirection and waste of scarce resources (H. Lee 1993). Such an arrangement would likely require that MFE allocate a certain percentage (perhaps 10 percent) of the total budget for science and technology activities to the PCST and the first senior presidential secretary for science and technology. The delegation of this budget authority is essential for the independence of technology policy planning and its success in directing and coordinating research and development efforts and applications.

On the surface, this appears to be a radical approach. It is difficult to imagine the president accepting a rigid hold on part of the overall budget which he must balance among all the competing budgetary interests. Cabinet-level politics will likely persist. The creation of a PCST chaired by the first senior presidential secretary for science and technology does not guarantee budget authority. Private sessions with the minister of MFE (which holds primary budget authority), the first senior presidential secretary for economic affairs, and the president will result in trade-offs with the PCST and the first senior presidential secretary for science and technology. The president, after all, has many deep interests and commitments—national defense, social development, international relations, etc.—that demand a priority for his budget. Yet such measures appear necessary to allow Korean technological growth. Perhaps the budget authority should be framed in terms of an investment in Korea's future. Pragmatically, the best way to assure that the PCST has budget influence rests on the relationship among the first senior presidential secretary for science and technology, the minister of MFE, and the first senior presidential secretary for economic affairs.

5

Shaping Development: Structural Determinants, Policy Choices, and Technology Transfer

Technology transfer is recognized as a major determinant in the fortunes of efforts by newly industrialized countries to foster economic development. There is also a growing realization that technology transfer is an important component for developed countries as well. Patterns of technology transfer are shaped in large part by associated policy strategies. For a newly industrialized state, fostering technology transfer is a balancing act. Technology importation can help industries accumulate technology in a short period of time. But by the same measure, states can expose themselves to foreign dominance in key sectoral areas. Technology transfer is also a balancing act for those states seeking to share technology with newly industrialized states. Transfer strategies can encourage the development of foreign markets, integrated development processes, and trade alliances. By transferring technology, however, the state runs the risk of giving away valuable resources, creating new competitors, and risking the loss of position in the global market (see Gilpin 1975; Kennedy 1987; Pollard 1985; Yoon 1990).

Given such opportunities and dangers, the path that the state seeks to pursue through technology-transfer policy becomes critical to the outcomes of technology transfer. Whether a state can pursue a consistent strategy over time, or have the ability to make corrections or anticipate adjustments, are substantial challenges facing those seeking to both export and import technologies. Overall, technology-transfer policy illustrates the interplay that takes place between structural conditions and the preferences of key decision makers in policy actions aimed at successfully acquiring, adopting, and absorbing technologies.

In large part, the purpose of this chapter is to illustrate the discretion that a host country can exert over technology transfer through various policy mechanisms. In particular, we explore four principal concerns: (1) the importance of the Korean government technology-transfer policy in technology-transfer patterns; (2) differences in the character and composition of technology transfer from the United States and Japan to Korean manufacturing industries; (3) identification of new policy challenges and their general implications in technology-transfer policy; and (4) the nature and limits of state policy intervention by the president and bureaucracy.[1] By presenting these four principal concerns, we are able to see how structural conditions have shaped and influenced policy actions. Our understanding of these concerns is also broadened by exploring the individual orientations, motives, and choices by key institutional players in the presidency and bureaucracy.

The idea that a state can consciously direct the course of technology development runs counter to the arguments of those who hold that economic development is more structurally deterministic: dependent on technological trends and the decisions of actors from abroad (for a discussion, see Lall 1993). For adherents of dependency theory, foreign direct investment may be acknowledged as a necessary transmission device to acquire technology to assist in economic development objectives. However, such arrangements pose the dangers of foreign control of domestic markets, absence of domestic production ownership, and resource exploitation (see O'Donnell 1973; Evans 1979). As we noted in chapter 2, the dependency perspective assumes the dominant influence of the donor country or firms over the developing host country. But this may not necessarily be the case. Indeed, the developing state may be able to exert influence on the pace, flow, and character of technology transfer.

By analyzing Korean technology-transfer policy experiences from 1962 to 1996—specifically two transfer practices, direct investment and technology licensing patterns from the United States and Japan to Korean manufacturing industries—we can evaluate the role that the developmental state has played in shaping industrialization. Such evaluation illustrates both the extent and the limit of state policy objectives and intervention. The prevailing view in much of the dependence and the neoclassical literature on international technology transfer from developed countries to developing countries has focused on the strong position of the former and the weak position of the latter.

In sharp contrast to this viewpoint, we find that the pattern and character of direct investment and technology licensing has been shaped, in large part, by technology-transfer policy strategies advanced and implemented by the Korean government. This finding is supported, in part, by analysis that reveals no substantial difference between Korea's principal sources of technology transfer—the United States and Japan—in distribution patterns of two transfer practices in Korean manufacturing industries. Contrasting with previous studies, these findings suggest that a host country's policy toward technology transfer can be a powerful determinant in patterns of technology transfer.

Finally, with the current pattern of industrialization and technological development, we argue that in the case of Korea the very same features of government technology-transfer policy that until the late 1980s were conducive for the rapid expansion of export-led industrialization now have become constraints to attempts to sustain industrialization through a technology-transfer arrangement. Since different stages in industrial and technological evolution call for different sets of technology-transfer policy, the dynamics and limits of state intervention and priorities are revealed.

Apart from evaluating the structural conditions that shape technology-transfer patterns and policy, we also consider the motives and relationships involved in individual actors who have a hand in technology policy. We are interested in both the presidency and the bureaucracy. As this chapter illustrates, technology-transfer policy experiences help to illuminate the priorities and orientations of the presidency and bureaucracy. Most importantly, for our purpose, the experience displays the tensions and dynamics involved in this institutional relationship. As we shall see, throughout the 1970s and into the 1980s, Korea's presidents often wanted immediate results to satisfy objectives outlined under ambitious five-year economic development plans. Foremost among these goals was to protect Korea's economy from being dominated by foreign competitors while successfully acquiring from abroad the technologies needed for industrialization. This led to very careful efforts to limit foreign direct investment and to implement technology licensing regulations. In more recent years, changes in technological needs and market conditions have forced a rethinking of policy approaches to technology transfer. As we saw in chapter 4, the growing complexity of technology transfer, absorption, and development places greater strength in the hands of the bureaucracy.

INTERNATIONAL POLITICAL ECONOMY OF TECHNOLOGY TRANSFER

There is an extensive body of theoretical and empirical literature on the effects of foreign investment on developing countries (Chenery and Strout 1966; Drysdale 1972; Griffin and Enos 1970; Helleiner 1989; Papanek 1973; Stobaugh and Wells 1984; Rosenstein-Rodan 1961; Weiskopf 1972). One current of the literature has focused on how foreign investment serves as a mechanism of technology transfer. From this perspective, foreign investment can be seen as a tool for economic development. But it is a tool not without its drawbacks. Given this, the appropriateness of the procedures by which technologies are transferred and the type of technologies transferred have been the subjects of wide inquiry. In regard to procedures, discussion has often focused on the relative merits of direct investment and technology-licensing arrangements. In regard to the substance of the technology transferred, questions have been raised about the level of sophistication and production factor intensity and how they relate to a host country's economic development goals (see Amsden 1987; Ferrantino 1992; Mardon 1990; Stobaugh and Wells 1984).

This question of appropriateness has often been at the center of research on the experiences of newly industrialized states in Asia. In such research, identification of distinctions between the technology-transfer practices of the United States and Japan, the two primary sources of technology in the Asian theater, have been given emphasis. For example, Kojima (1973, 1977, 1978, 1985) and Ozawa (1979) argued that Japanese technology-transfer policies are more appropriate to developing countries than those of the United States (see Yoon 1990). This is based on the observation that technologies transferred from Japan have a better "fit" with the needs of developing countries in terms of accessibility, standardization, and maturation. In other words, technology transfer from Japan lends itself to assimilation. On the other hand, American technology-transfer practices have been seen as detrimental because they tend to be patented, high-level technology, and sophisticated. Such technologies are not easily diffused in a developing host country, leading to the establishment of an enclave with little linkage to the rest of the economy. In Kojima's argument, the appropriateness of a technology is a matter of the degree of technological sophistication—it should match the needs of the recipient country, not the interests of the foreign investor. Furthermore, as Lee (1984) points out, Kojima's argument implies that technology transfer from Japan tends to concentrate on the labor-intensive, low-technology industries (for definitions see note 13). In comparison, technology transfer from the United States tends to concentrate on the capital-intensive, high-technology industries.[2] Kojima (1985) found support for his hypothesis from the experiences of seven developing Asian states, including Korea.

The idea that the Japanese model of technology transfer is preferable for developing countries has generated considerable commentary in the literature. Some concede that Kojima's and Ozawa's hypothesis might be true in explaining patterns of U.S. and Japanese foreign investments in the 1960s and early 1970s, but caution that the hypothesis loses explanatory power in comparing patterns in the late 1970s and the 1980s (see Clark and Chan 1995). Disputing Kojima's and Ozawa's views, some argue that the Japanese pattern is neither the result of a coordinated policy strategy nor reflective of an economic or social disposition toward sharing mature and standardized technologies. To the contrary, some scholars argue that earlier patterns in Japanese technology transfer were a fortuitous circumstance and reflect its then-limited industrial and economic capacity to export technology (Dunning 1988; Mason 1980; Roemer 1975, 1976; Yoon 1990). In other words, Japan is just a latecomer to both foreign investment and the creation of technology. To test Kojima's hypothesis, especially in Korea, Lee (1984) compared technologies transferred from Japan and the United States to Korean manufacturing industries in terms of levels of technological sophistication from 1962–1978. Challenging Kojima's findings, Lee (1984) found that there was no difference in the distribution of technology transfer from the United States and Japan to Korea, with the exception of the initial takeoff period of development running from 1962 to 1972. (Within this period, the only differences were in terms of direct investment.)

As we noted earlier, implicit in these arguments is the assumption of a clearly dominant relationship of the donor country to the developing host country. Under these arguments, developing countries who play host to the transfer of technologies from foreign donors are seen to be dependent and to have little room for discretion and control in shaping patterns of technology transfer. In contrast with these views, other studies argue that a host country's policy toward technology transfer can be a powerful determinant in patterns of technology transfer (Chou 1988; Haggard 1990; Hahm, Plein, and Florida 1994; Kim and Dahlman 1992; Mardon 1990; Mardon and Paik 1992). In this regard, the Korean experience in technology transfer provides a new perspective on the relationship between what has generally been thought of as the weak host in contrast to the strong donor and on the debate about the nature of the developmental state in transition.

There exist useful studies relating to the influence of Korean government policy on patterns of technology transfer to Korea from the United States and Japan (Coolidge 1981; Haggard 1990; Mardon 1990; Mardon and Paik 1992; Pack and Westphal 1986; Westphal, Kim, and Dahlman 1985). However, there are compelling methodological and substantive reasons to continue inquiry into this subject. First, prior research has generally overlooked the effect of rapid changes in various aspects of the Korean government policy on technology transfer. In particular, government policy has played an important role in shaping technology transfer. Second, the availability of recent data now allows the opportunity to explore the nature of longitudinal developments in the pattern and character of technology transfer in conjunction with the influence of government's technology-transfer planning and policy from 1962 through the mid-1990s. Third, and most importantly, this topic clearly displays the role of the developmental state and its limitation of the postdevelopmental state in guiding the course of economic expansion.

GOVERNMENT POLICY AND EMPIRICAL PATTERNS OF TECHNOLOGY TRANSFER

A brief historical review of Korean technology policy helps put industrial development into perspective. The Korean experience reveals the links between industrialization planning and technology-development policies in economic-development strategies (Chin 1986; Choi 1986; Kim and Dahlman 1992). Through the use of five-year economic development plans, Korea embarked on an effort to shape the course of foreign investment. The First and Second Five-Year Economic and Social Development Plans (FYESDP), covering the period from 1962 through 1971, marked the takeoff stage for industrialization in Korea. During this period, Korea was almost completely dependent on the help of developed nations in the area of production facilities and technologies. Emphasis was placed on fostering strategic import-substitution industries such as energy, fertilizer, and cement, while focusing on the development of export-oriented light industries. At this time, primary emphasis was placed on the importation of technologies for application in industrial production processes.

The 1970s and early 1980s, particularly during the Third and Fourth FYESDPs (1972 through 1981) can be considered the growth stage of Korean industrialization. During this period, emphasis was placed on building an industrial foundation by fostering a select group of industries, including machinery, metals, chemicals, shipbuilding, and electronics. This stage was characterized by the effort to go one step beyond importing foreign technologies. Serious efforts were made to enhance imported technologies and to upgrade domestic capabilities to absorb these technologies. By the late 1980s, Korea's strategy for technological development was beginning to bear fruit. It achieved a virtually independent capacity for development in light industry. Korea had also achieved a level of minimal dependence on foreign technology in heavy and chemical industries. With the Fifth and Sixth FYESDPs (1982 through 1991), the development of strategic industries was targeted, with focus given to developing indigenous technologies and acquiring new knowledge-intensive industries.

Since the launching of the First FYESDP in 1962, when real postwar reconstruction was initiated, Korean technology-transfer policies have primarily taken two channels. One has been direct investment, which, as the name implies, involves the direct participation of foreign firms in domestic sectors of the economy. The second has been technology licensing, which involves arrangements whereby royalties are paid to utilize technologies developed by foreign firms. Many researchers argue that both of these paths of development have been shaped in large part by conscious policy actions of the Korean government (Coolidge 1981; Hahm, Plein, and Florida 1994; Kim and Dahlman 1992; Pack and

Westphal 1986; Westphal, Kim, and Dahlman 1985; Yu 1986). However, it is very difficult to identify the factors that enable us to determine the pattern of technology transfer. Possible factors include macroeconomic performance, international economic environments, government policy, big business interests, etc. Therefore, it is necessary to consider these in terms of an interacting combination of factors within which causal priority is difficult to determine. Understanding these factors is analogous to the opening of a combination lock rather than a padlock. In short, the extent of policy influence on the pattern of technology transfer is of special interest.

Direct Investments

Over the course of the past two decades, Korea's government policy on direct investments has seen dramatic swings to adjust to new market realities and new domestic capabilities.[3] For example, reflecting the need to quickly acquire technological know-how and to spur industrial development, Korea pursued a liberal policy on direct investment during the 1960s. Any form of bona fide foreign capital, including fully owned subsidiaries, was courted by offering extensive incentives. In order to encourage foreign direct investment and minimize regulatory obstacles, the Korean government implemented the Foreign Investment Encouragement Law in 1960. Provisions of the law included such incentives as a five-year tax holiday, duty-free status for imported machinery and raw materials used as manufacturing capital, and protection against foreign property expropriation by the state (Yang 1972: 244). In 1966, incentives under the Foreign Investment Encouragement Law were strengthened with the passage of the Foreign Capital Inducement Law. The same year, the Office of Investment Promotion was created to respond to the information needs and inquiries of foreign investors (Yang 1972:245). But by the 1970s, this situation had changed. The government reversed its policy on direct investment and tightened control; for example, joint ventures received higher priority than wholly owned subsidiaries. This reflected the Korean government's view that industrial development had reached a point of domestic capacity to absorb and assimilate relatively mature technologies. The prevailing viewpoint during this time was that continued direct investment would constrain autonomous industrial development.

TABLE 5.1. Direct Investment by Economic Sector (Cases/$1,000)

	1962–1976	1977–1981	1982–1993.1	Total	Percent
Agriculture, Fisheries, & Mining	83 (14,672)	14 (6,421)	28 (32,444)	125 (53,537)	3.2 (0.5)
Manufacturing	1,070 (907,609)	191 (482,161)	1,560 (5,480,446)	2,829 (6,870,716)	72.1 (67.5)
Food Processing	37 (23,419)	13 (39,025)	120 (367,823)	170 (426,267)	4.3 (4.2)
Textiles	150 (189,609)	10 (4,981)	83 (115,426)	243 (310,016)	6.2 (3.0)
Paper & Wood Products	24 (6,908)	6 (6,491)	25 (147,746)	55 (161,145)	1.4 (1.6)
Chemicals	115 (196,119)	20 (140,738)	235 (128,079.7)	370 (1,617,654)	9.4 (15.9)
Fertilizer	5 (45,825)	– (1,500)	2 (1,496)	7 (48,821)	0.2 (0.5)
Medical Products	19 (6,171)	9 (14,521)	53 (329,736)	81 (350,428)	2.1 (3.4)
Petroleum	17 (75,207)	2 (9,515)	4 (567,571)	13 (654,298)	0.3 (6.4)
Ceramics	41 (20,698)	7 (5,730)	32 (123,032)	80 (149,460)	2.0 (1.5)
Metals	86 (63,999)	21 (36,097)	84 (104,780)	191 (204,876)	4.9 (2.0)
Machinery	139 (61,522)	47 (58,081)	329 (510,034)	507 (629,637)	12.9 (6.2)
Electronics & Electricity	253 (149,439)	31 (124,394)	321 (1,125,620)	605 (1,399,453)	15.4 (13.7)

As illustrated in Table 5.1, the composition of foreign direct investments by economic sector further illustrates the distribution of funding since 1962. After the adoption of the First FYESDP in 1962, direct investments increased in Korea. As Table 5.1 indicates, foreign direct investments have been concentrated for the most part in manufacturing (representing 72.1 percent of all cases

TABLE 5.1. Continued.

	1962–1976	1977–1981	1982–1993.1	Total	Percent
Transportation	25 (43,802)	11 (38,645)	97 (725,592)	133 (808,039)	3.4 (7.9)
Other	169 (24,891)	14 (6,443)	191 (79,288)	314 (110,622)	9.5 (1.1)
Service	87 (223,175)	34 (232,067)	845 (2,808,444)	971 (3,264,186)	24.7 (32.1)
Construction	3 (3,680)	1 (9,800)	10 (43,822)	14 (57,302)	0.4 (0.6)
Wholesale/Retail	–	–	48 (66,524)	48 (66,524)	0.1 (0.7)
Trade	3 (52)	3 (358)	388 (256,059)	394 (256,469)	10.0 (2.5)
Food	–	1 (100)	38 (30,781)	39 (30,881)	0.1 (0.3)
Hotel	34 (168,557)	11 (71,314)	33 (1,530,527)	78 (1,770,398)	2.0 (17.4)
Transportation	11 (7,332)	3 (23,183)	29 (19,978)	43 (50,493)	1.1 (0.5)
Finance	7 (13,362)	7 (90,778)	47 (521,974)	61 (626,114)	1.6 (6.1)
Insurance	–	3 (3,009)	11 (182,422)	14 (185,431)	0.44 (1.8)
Other	29 (30,192)	10 (33,525)	241 (156,857)	280 (220,574)	0.7 (2.2)
Total	1,240 (1,145,456)	244 (720,649)	2,441 (8,322,334)	3,925 (10,188,439)	

(Source: Korean Economic Planning Board, "The Current State of Foreign Investment," Seoul, 1993)

and 67.5 percent of the value of direct investments). Manufacturing investments have been heavily concentrated in electronics and electricity, machinery, and chemicals; together they account for 37.7 percent (35.8 percent) of total direct investments, or 52 percent (53 percent) of total manufacturing direct investments.

In terms of sectoral composition, during the 1962–1976 period, direct investment was channeled into the development of chemicals; textiles; electronics and electricity; machinery; metals; and agriculture, fisheries, and mining. These sectors contained 67 percent (60 percent in terms of value) of all 1,240 ($1.15 billion) direct investments in Korea. During the 1977–1981 period, direct investment was channeled into the development of chemicals, electronics and electricity, machinery, and metals. These sectors contained 49 percent (50 percent) of all 244 ($0.7 billion) direct investments. During the 1982–1993.1 period, direct investment was channeled into the development of electronics and electricity, transportation, machinery, chemicals, medical products, food processing, ceramics, and metals. These sectors contained 52 percent (41 percent) of all 2,441 ($8.3 billion) direct investments. As indicated in Haggard (1990) and Mardon (1990), this sectoral composition of direct investments closely conforms with state strategies of industrial development. In short, this sectoral composition reflects the steady transformation of the Korean economy to more sophisticated industries. Mardon (1990) argues that direct investments in these areas have played a significant role in Korean industrialization by providing foreign-exchange-earning exports or technologies for import substitution that have created necessary linkages for domestic industrial producers. Similarly, Ernst (1994) argues that during the critical early phase of the development of the electronics industry, by opening up export channels for assembled chips and for simple consumer devices, direct investments played an important catalytic role.

These empirical patterns also clearly display the influence of government policy toward direct investment. For example, even considering the greater demand for technologies from rapid structural development of the Korean economy, total foreign direct investment during the 1977–1981 period is only 244 cases, compared with 1,240 during the 1962–1976 period and 2,441 during the 1982–1993.1 period. Disaggregating the period of most rapid growth (1962–1976), we see 39 cases ($0.05 billion) from 1961–1966, 350 ($0.22 billion) from 1967–1971, and 851 ($0.88 billion) from 1972–1976. In the subsequent periods, we find 244 ($0.73 billion) from 1977–1981, 565 ($1.8 billion) from 1982–1986, and 1,335 ($4.2 billion) from 1987–1990. These patterns are closely related to the restricted government policy on direct investments

TABLE 5.2A.   Total Cases of Direct Investments from Japan and the
United States in Korea: 1962–January 31, 1993 (cases)

Period	Japan	U.S.	Subtotal	Others	Total
1962–1971	246	110	356	43	399
1972–1981	871	145	1,016	102	1,118
1982–1991	1,061	632	1,693	561	2,254
1992–Jan 31, 1993	80	73	153	104	257
1962–Jan 31, 1993	2,258	960	3,218	810	4,028
	(56%)	(24%)	(80%)	(20%)	(100%)

(**Source:** Korean Economic Planning Board, "The Current State of Foreign
Investment," Seoul, 1993)

during the period of 1977–1981[4] and also to the liberalized government policy on the acceleration of investment after 1982. The
overall trend seems to follow the rapid development of the
Korean economy and government policy over direct investments.
A positive investment climate in the 1980s and the loosening of
restrictions on direct investment in 1984 no doubt contributed to
the accelerated pattern in the 1980s and the early 1990s (Hahm,
Plein, and Florida 1994; Kim and Dahlman 1992; Mardon 1990;
Yu 1986).

Despite this growth, as a proportion of total foreign capital
inflow between 1962 and 1984, the share of direct investments in
Korea remained low, averaging approximately 5 percent of the
total capital inflow (Korean Economic Planning Board 1985).[5]
Indeed, yearly data from 1987 to 1992 reveal a substantial decline
of direct investments in terms of both cases and dollar values in
the manufacturing sector, particularly after 1987.[6] This substantial decline calls for a different set of technology-transfer policies.
We return to this observation later in our discussion.

Given that Japan and the United States have been the principal
sources of technology transfer to Korea, examination of patterns
of direct investment from these two donor states deserve attention. Tables 5.2A and 5.2B illustrate Korea's accelerated pace of
direct investment in technology transfer in the first twenty years
of its economic development initiatives. These tables display patterns in the number and amounts of direct investments from
Japan and the United States, respectively. Between 1962 and end of

TABLE 5.2B. Total Amounts of Direct Investments from Japan and the United States in Korea: 1962–January 31, 1993 ($1,000)

Period	Japan	U.S.	Subtotal	Others	Total
1962–1971	98,017	120,324	218,341	47,690	266,031
1972–1981	927,910	370,615	798,525	801,549	1,600,074
1982–1991	2,993,007	2,063,720	5,056,727	2,345,968	7,402,695
1992–Jan 31, 1993	156,249	390,125	546,374	373,265	919,639
1962–Jan 31, 1993	4,180,382	2,939,585	7,119,967	3,068,472	10,188,439
	(41%)	(29%)	(70%)	(30%)	(100%)

(**Source:** Korean Economic Planning Board, "The Current State of Foreign Investment," Seoul, 1993)

January 1993 there were 2,258 direct investments from Japan, amounting to a total of approximately $4.18 billion, and 960 direct investments from the United States, amounting to approximately $2.9 billion. Direct investments from Japan and the United States together account for 80 percent of total cases[7] and 70 percent of total amount. These patterns clearly show that Japan and the United States are the two major investors in Korea.

Tables 5.2A and 5.2B reveal an interesting wrinkle in the pattern of direct-investment arrangements between Korean firms and Japan and the United States. While the total number of direct investments from the United States is smaller than that from Japan over time, the average value per case of Japanese direct investment is well below that from the United States. The average value per case of direct investment from the United States is $3.02 million, whereas the average value per case of direct investment from Japan is $1.85 million. However, as can be seen in Table 5.2B, because of the many factors influencing cost differentials, such as geographic distance, and the lack of detailed data on the actual value of specific cases of direct investment, we cannot assume that U.S. firms were transferring different and more valuable technology than Japanese firms.

Overall, the data illustrate the dynamics of direct-investment flows over time. We argue that much of this is attributable to Korean policy decisions. For example, foreign direct-investment rates changed during the 1980s as the government gradually reversed restrictions and substantially relaxed direct-investment guidelines to adjust to changes in the global marketplace. Korea liberalized its direct-investment policy in 1984 when it removed all significant legal barriers to direct investment and reiterated its open invitation to increased direct investment. Despite these efforts, however, the overall level of direct investment remains relatively low compared with other newly industrialized countries, and Korea remains essentially isolated from the more dynamic aspects of direct investments (see Kim and Dahlman 1992; Mardon 1990; Westphal, Kim, and Dahlman 1985; Yu 1986). Moreover, afraid that Korea might become a competitor, foreign sources were reluctant to grant licenses for high technologies, particularly for knowledge-intensive industry. As a result, the Korean government turned to more open direct-investment schemes in 1994 to attract the transfer of more advanced technologies.

Technology Licensing

In the case of Korea, the major source of technology for large firms took the form of technology licensing. As Kim and Dahlman (1992), Mardon (1990), Westphal, Kim, and Dahlman (1985), and others point out, there are a number of reasons for this. First, technology licensing is seen as a means of effectively securing established technological processes which shorten the lead time for industrial start-up. Second, considering long-standing tensions with North Korea, Korea has not always been viewed as an attractive location for direct investment. In the past, some foreign investors have considered it better to limit direct investment to low-technology, footloose industries or pursue licensing arrangements than to commit to heavily capitalized investments. Third, Korea has tended to have a negative view toward direct investment because of the potential for foreign dominance in the domestic economy. This viewpoint has been particularly pronounced in the case of Japanese investment. To facilitate the development of domestic production and to reduce the level of penetration of foreign direct investment, technology licensing arrangements are used to preserve the host country's control over the presence of foreign interests (Mardon 1990). According to Mardon (1990:121), "Foreign direct investment was preferred and sought after only if it could provide a technology that was necessary to develop a targeted sector, and if that technology was not available domestically or through a technological license." In terms of number of cases, these arrangements account for almost half of formal technology importation.

Technology licensing (TL) was initiated in 1962. Through the mid-1960s, Korean policy was quite restrictive in terms of royalty ceilings and duration of licensing arrangements (for further details on legal and bureaucratic control mechanisms over technology licensing, see Yu 1986).[8] In the early years of industrialization, acquisition of high technology was not a critical element in economic development. Instead, emphasis was placed on securing highly mature technologies that were available "off the shelf" to aid in such established industries as plywood, shoes, and textiles. Highly mature technologies could be more easily acquired through mechanisms other than TL (see Pack and Westphal 1986; Westphal, Kim, Dahlman 1985). With a more secure footing in developing an industrial base and demand for relatively mature technologies, such as consumer electronics, the 1970s saw significant change in Korean TL policy (Kim and Dahlman 1992). Restrictions on TL were relaxed in 1970 and 1978 (see Westphal, Kim, and Dahlman 1985; and Yu 1986 for details). The policy was further relaxed in 1984 by procedural changes in TL arrangements, which shifted emphasis from an approval system to a reporting system (see Korean Ministry of Science and Technology 1986b).

As Table 5.3 indicates, like patterns of direct investments, TL for manufacturing has been heavily concentrated in electronics and electricity, machinery, and oil refining and chemicals; together they account for 67.3 percent (73.6 percent of value) of TL. Again, all of these three industries have been designated as target sectors by the government. In terms of sectoral composition, during the 1962–1976 period TL was channeled into the development of machinery, electronics and electricity, oil refining and chemicals, and metals. These sectors contained 74 percent (74 percent) of all 752 ($0.13 billion) TL in Korea. During the 1977–1981 period, TL was channeled into the development of oil refining and chemicals, machinery, electronics and electricity, synthetic fibers, metals, ceramics, shipbuilding, and food processing. These sectors contained 74 percent (70 percent) of all 1,225 ($0.45 billion) technology licensing arrangements. During the 1982–1993.2 period, TL was channeled into the development of electronics and electricity, machinery, oil refining and chemicals, synthetic fibers, and metals. These sectors contained 87 percent (84 percent) of all

TABLE 5.3. Technology Licensing by Economic Sector (Cases/$1,000)

	1962–1976	1977–1981	1982–1993.2	Total	Percent
Agriculture & Dairy Farming	6 (2,038.6)	5 (4,561.9)	26 (13,032.7)	37 (19,633.2)	0.4 (0.3)
Food Processing	15 (2,039.5)	30 (3,311.1)	211 (69,203.3)	256 (74,553.9)	3.1 (1.1)
Pulp and Paper Manufacturing	17 (111.7)	7 (7,353.2)	15 (8,634.6)	27 (16,099.5)	0.3 (0.2)
Textiles	17 (664.1)	12 (4,910.7)	34 (14,606.1)	63 (20,180.9)	0.7 (0.3)
Synthetic Fibers	21 (8,700.6)	29 (13,367.2)	340 (104,455.7)	390 (126,523.5)	4.8 (1.8)
Ceramics & Cement	21 (1,040.6)	34 (10,565.1)	109 (125,888.3)	224 (137,494.0)	2.7 (2.0)
Oil Refinery and Chemicals	149 (32,631.4)	194 (147,275.3)	1,205 (975,711.6)	1,348 (1,155,618.3)	16.5 (16.3)
Pharmaceuticals	27 (1,184.4)	31 (649.6)	142 (54,107.3)	200 (55,941.3)	2.5 (0.8)
Metals	74 (23,906.1)	105 (31,976.4)	246 (94,276.8)	425 (150,159.3)	5.2 (2.1)
Electronics and Electricity	154 (12,801.8)	205 (47,461.6)	1,665 (2,577,889.5)	2,024 (2,638,152.9)	24.8 (37.1)
Machinery	180 (14,566.5)	403 (89,329.1)	1,538 (1,314,436.9)	2,121 (1,418,332.5)	26.0 (20.2)
Ship Building	11 (5,091.0)	45 (11,272.9)	169 (179,372.3)	225 (195,736.2)	2.8 (2.8)
Communications	26 (5,033.4)	21 (18,700.3)	56 (84,550.1)	113 (108,283.8)	1.4 (1.5)
Electric Power Generation	9 (2,759.0)	37 (25,416.0)	47 (666,768.9)	93 (694,943.9)	0.1 (10.0)
Construction	8 (248.2)	25 (17,707.1)	100 (36,484.2)	133 (54,439.5)	1.6 (0.7)
Others	27 (725.6)	42 (17,534.0)	397 (193,990.8)	466 (212,250.4)	5.7 (3.0)
Total	752 (113,542.5)	1,225 (451,391.5)	6,170 (6,513,409.1)	8,147 (7,078,343.1)	

(**Source:** Korean Ministry of Finance, "Trends in Technology Inducement," Seoul, 1993)

Table 5.4A.   Technology Licensing from Japan and the United States: 1962–February 28, 1993 (cases)

Period	Japan	U.S.	Subtotal	Others	Total
1962–1966	11	13	24	9	33
1967–1971	203	61	264	21	285
1972–1976	280	90	370	64	434
1977–1981	631	302	933	292	1,225
1982–1986	1,074	515	1,589	489	2,078
1987–1991	1,613	1,010	2,623	848	3,471
1992–Feb 28, 1993	272	188	460	161	621
1962–Feb 28, 1993	4,084	2,179	6,263	1,884	8,147
	(50%)	(27%)	(77%)	(23%)	(100%)

(**Source:** Korean Ministry of Finance, "Trends in Technology Inducement," Seoul, 1993)

6,170 ($6.5 billion) TL. Like patterns of direct investments, patterns in TL arrangements reflect the steady transformation of the Korean economy and government policy regarding technology licensing, which placed growing emphasis on acquiring more sophisticated technologies over the thirty-year period (Yu 1986).

As in the case of direct investment, the major players have been Japan and the United States. From 1962 to February 28, 1993, the number of TL from Japan was 4,084, and the amount of royalty payments over $2.2 billion. During the same time period, the number of TL from the United States was 2,179, with royalty payments amounting to over $3.4 billion.[9] The total number of TL from and the total amount of the royalty payments to Japan and the United States amounted to 6,263 (87 percent of the total TL) and $5,632 million (80 percent of the total royalty payments). This clearly shows that the sources of TL are heavily inclined toward these two countries. Tables 5.4A and 5.4B illustrate the pattern of technology licensing arrangements from Japan and the United States since 1962.

As shown in Tables 5.4A and 5.4B, the number of TL cases jumped from 33 in the first FYESDP (1962–1966) to 434 a decade later (1972–1976), to 2,078 (1982–1986), and to 3,471 in the 1987–1991 period.[10] The total TL as of February 28, 1993, amounted to

Table 5.4B. Royalty Payments for Technology Licensing from Japan and the United States: 1962–February 28, 1993 ($1 million)

Period	Japan	U.S.	Subtotal	Others	Total
1962–1966	–	0.6	0.6	0.2	0.8
1967–1971	50	7.8	12.8	3.5	16.3
1972–1976	587	21.3	80	16.5	96.5
1977–1981	139.8	159.2	299	152.4	451.4
1982–1986	323.7	602.8	426.5	258.4	1,184.9
1987–1991	1,382	2,121.6	3,503.6	855.7	4,359.3
1992–Feb 28, 1993	297.9	511.7	809.6	159.4	969
1962–Feb 28, 1993	2,207.1	3,424.9	5,632.0	1,446.3	7,078.3
	(31%)	(49%)	(80%)	(20%)	(100%)

(**Source:** Korean Ministry of Finance, "Trends in Technology Inducement," Seoul, 1993)

8,147 cases or $7.1 billion in royalty payments. The last period (1987–February 28, 1993) accounts for over 50 percent of total cases. Similarly, as indicated in Table 5.4B, royalty payments also rose dramatically in the 1980s and early 1990s. The last period accounts for 75 percent of cumulative royalty payments ($5.3 billion). This TL pattern illustrates how technologies have been imported more actively in recent years. The liberalization policy regarding TL has had considerable influence on this increase (Hahm, Plein, and Florida 1994; Yu 1986). Under these new arrangements, rather than seeking the blessing of the state, private interests could engage in TL as long as they abided by reporting procedures.

As compared with direct investments, technology-licensing arrangements appear to be more sensitive to policy controls and under the influence of external technological and market forces. Because of the nature of their fixed terms and royalty arrangements, technology licensing is easier to control than direct investments, which require longer-term commitments and guarantees to the donor. From a market and technological perspective, some technologies lend themselves more readily to licensing than others. For donors, for example, production-oriented processes based on machinery and sophisticated techniques are more attractive to license. On the other hand, knowledge-intensive processes, such as software and biomedical technologies, are more easily diffused and altered, raising proprietary concerns for donors. We will return to this point later in our discussion.

TECHNOLOGY TRANSFER FROM THE UNITED STATES AND JAPAN IN KOREAN MANUFACTURING INDUSTRIES

In order to evaluate arguments about appropriate models of technology transfer and to illustrate the level of influence that host state policy has on technology-transfer patterns, we now turn to a comparison of technology-transfer flows from Japan and the United States. It is difficult to obtain a direct measure of the distribution pattern of technologies transferred through direct investments, technology licensing, and other mechanisms, since technology is an inseparable part of the bundle of factors transferred through a variety of channels (Kim and Dahlman 1992; Lee 1984). Even if it could be unbundled from other factors, there is no established unit for measuring a technology transfer. Therefore, following Lee (1984), we use direct investments and technology licensing based on the number of cases[11] as indicators of the distribution pattern of technology transfers in this analysis.[12]

The distribution patterns of these direct investments among the four industry groups are reported in terms of cases and values in Tables 5.5A and 5.5B, respectively.[13] Direct investments from Japan in Korean manufacturing have been concentrated in the capital-intensive, high-technology industries. This holds for both the number of cases and values of direct investment. Direct investments from the United States also concentrate in the capital-intensive, high-technology industries, but to a stronger extent (44 percent; 60 percent). Furthermore, when we group direct investments between the low-technology and the high-technology industries, we find no strong differences in the distribution pattern of direct investments between Japan and the United States in terms of both cases and dollar values. Direct investments from both countries are concentrated in the high-technology industries, although when compared to each other, the United States edges out Japan slightly.[14]

These results contrast with the findings of Kojima (1973, 1977, 1978, 1985), Ozawa (1979), and Lee (1980), who argue that direct investments from Japan concentrate in the low-technology

TABLE 5.5A.   Distribution Pattern of Direct Investments from
Japan and the United States in Korean Manufacturing Industries:
1962–January 31, 1993

Direct Investments from Japan
cases (%)

Industries	Low-Technology	High-Technology	Subtotal
Labor-Intensive	603	416	1,019
	(31%)	(22%)	(53%)
Capital-Intensive	269	635	904
	(14%)	(33%)	(47%)
Subtotal	872	1,051	1,923
	(45%)	(55%)	(100%)

(**Note:** Service industries and others are 335; therefore, the total is 2,258.)

Direct Investments from the United States
cases (%)

Industries	Low-Technology	High-Technology	Subtotal
Labor-Intensive	179	133	312
	(28%)	(20%)	(48%)
Capital-Intensive	55	283	338
	(8%)	(44%)	(52%)
Subtotal	234	416	650
	(36%)	(64%)	(100%)

(**Note:** Service industries and others are 310; therefore, the total is 960.)

industries while direct investments from the United States concentrate in the high-technology industries in Korea.[15] These patterns can be seen as evidence of the rapid structural transformation of Korean industrialization, bringing about greater and greater demand for high technologies. As we noted earlier, these patterns also can be seen as a consequence of Korean government policy on direct investments for the development of high-technology industries.

The figures in Table 5.5A, which are cumulative cases for the 1962–January 31, 1993, period, do not inform us whether or not

TABLE 5.5B.   Distribution Pattern of Direct Investments from Japan and the United States in Korean Manufacturing Industries: 1962–January 31, 1993 (based on values)

Direct Investments from Japan
$1,000 (%)

Industries	Low-Technology	High-Technology	Subtotal
Labor-Intensive	420,287 (19%)	598,806 (27%)	1,019,093 (45%)
Capital-Intensive	189,431 (8%)	1,034,870 (46%)	1,224,301 (55%)
Subtotal	609,718 (27%)	1,633,676 (73%)	2,243,394 (100%)

Direct Investments from the United States
$1,000 (%)

Industries	Low-Technology	High-Technology	Subtotal
Labor-Intensive	192,567 (8%)	583,658 (24%)	776,225 (32%)
Capital-Intensive	194,597 (8%)	1,463,887 (60%)	1,658,484 (68%)
Subtotal	387,164 (16%)	2,047,545 (84%)	2,434,709 (100%)

there is any change in the type of direct investments relating to the structural transformation of the Korean economy and Korean government policy over the course of the period. As Lee (1984) argues, by the early 1970s Korea was well on its way to rapid industrialization characterized by a strategic transition from labor-intensive, low-technology industries to labor- or capital-intensive, high-technology industries such as the heavy and chemical industries. Moreover, from the early 1980s Korean technology development focused on new knowledge-intensive industries, including biotechnology, computers, semiconductors, and telecommunications. It is

TABLE 5.6A.   Distribution Pattern of Direct Investments from
Japan and the United States in Korean Manufacturing Industries:
1962–1972

Direct Investments from Japan
cases (%)

Industries	Low-Technology	High-Technology	Subtotal
Labor-Intensive	40 (48%)	21 (25%)	61 (73%)
Capital-Intensive	14 (17%)	9 (11%)	23 (27%)
Subtotal	54 (64%)	30 (36%)	84 (100%)

Direct Investments from the United States
cases (%)

Industries	Low-Technology	High-Technology	Subtotal
Labor-Intensive	14 (39%)	12 (33%)	26 (72%)
Capital-Intensive	4 (11%)	6 (17%)	10 (28%)
Subtotal	18 (50%)	18 (50%)	36 (100%)

therefore possible that in the early 1970s and 1980s there were
changes in the distribution pattern of direct investments from
Japan and the United States.

   In order to test this argument, we divided the period into
1962–1972, 1973–1978, and 1979–January 31, 1993, and analyzed
the distribution pattern of direct investments from Japan and the
United States for these three subperiods. Consistent with Lee
(1980), Table 5.6A clearly shows that during the first subperiod
direct investments from both Japan (48 percent) and the United

TABLE 5.6B. Distribution Pattern of Direct Investments from Japan and the United States in Korean Manufacturing Industries: 1973–1978

Direct Investments from Japan
cases (%)

Industries	Low-Technology	High-Technology	Subtotal
Labor-Intensive	60 (18%)	188 (57%)	248 (75%)
Capital-Intensive	32 (10%)	49 (15%)	81 (27%)
Subtotal	92 (28%)	237 (72%)	329 (100%)

Direct Investments from the United States
cases (%)

Industries	Low-Technology	High-Technology	Subtotal
Labor-Intensive	6 (19%)	13 (41%)	19 (60%)
Capital-Intensive	1 (3%)	12 (38%)	13 (40%)
Subtotal	7 (22%)	25 (78%)	32 (100%)

States (39 percent) were concentrated in the labor-intensive, low-technology industries, with Japan being more so concentrated. During this time, firms in both Japan and the United States looked to Korea as a source of cheap labor for manufacturing and assembly production (Westphal, Kim, and Dahlman 1985; Ernst 1994).

As shown in Table 5.6B, during the period of 1973–1978 direct investments from both Japan (57 percent) and the United States (41 percent) were concentrated in the labor-intensive, high-technology industries, Japan being the more concentrated.[16] These

TABLE 5.6C. Distribution Pattern of Direct Investments from Japan and the United States in Korean Manufacturing Industries: 1979–January 21, 1993

Direct Investments from Japan
cases (%)

Industries	Low-Technology	High-Technology	Subtotal
Labor-Intensive	503 (33%)	207 (14%)	710 (47%)
Capital-Intensive	223 (15%)	577 (38%)	800 (53%)
Subtotal	726 (48%)	784 (52%)	1,510 (100%)

Direct Investments from the United States
cases (%)

Industries	Low-Technology	High-Technology	Subtotal
Labor-Intensive	159 (27%)	108 (19%)	267 (46%)
Capital-Intensive	50 (9%)	265 (45%)	315 (54%)
Subtotal	209 (36%)	373 (64%)	582 (100%)

results are a marked contrast with those of Kojima (1977, 1978, 1985) and Ozawa (1979) but are consistent with Lee (1984). These results reflect, in part, a commitment by the Korean government to initiate policies aimed at facilitating the development of a domestic high-technology industrial base.

Table 5.6C, however, indicates an important shift in these patterns. During the period of 1979-January 31, 1993, direct investments from Japan (38 percent) and the United States (45 percent) concentrated in the capital-intensive, high-technology industries. This analysis reveals major changes in the distribution pattern of direct investments from Japan and the United States to Korea. Direct investment from both Japan and the United States concentrated in the labor-intensive, low-technology industries only during the 1962–1972 subperiod and in the labor-intensive, high-technology industries during the 1973–1978 subperiod. Since 1979, direct investments from both Japan and the United States have concentrated in the capital-intensive, high-technology industries. These trends reflect, in part, changes in Korean policy aimed at nurturing and sustaining what was becoming a relatively sophisticated technology base.

Through analysis of these subperiods, in contrast with Kojima (1977, 1978, 1985) and Ozawa (1979) but consistent with Roemer (1975, 1976), we find no substantial difference between Japan and the United States in distribution patterns of investments in Korean manufacturing industries. Moreover, Korean government policy and industrial and economic conditions are determinant factors in distribution patterns of direct investment. In particular, these patterns may be the result of a policy emphasis on selective restriction in direct investment (Hahm, Plein, and Florida 1994; Kim and Dahlman 1992; Mardon 1990; Mardon and Paik 1992; Yu 1986).[17] The patterns of direct investment across the three subperiods illustrated here display the influence of the policy aims of each Five-Year Economic and Social Development Plan.

Table 5.7 shows that patterns in the distribution of technology licensing from Japan to Korean manufacturing industries tend to concentrate in the capital-intensive, high-technology industries (49 percent). TL from the US also concentrates in the capital-intensive, high-technology industries (63 percent), but to a greater extent. When we group TL into the low-technology and the high-technology industries, we find no strong difference in the TL distribution pattern between Japan and the United States. TL from both countries are strongly concentrated in the high-technology industries.

When TL are divided between the labor-intensive and the capital-intensive industries, TL from Japan and the United States are both concentrated in the capital-intensive industries (although, when compared to each other, the United States has a slight lead over Japan in these arrangements). These results contrast with the conclusions of Kojima (1977), who argues that the United States transfers new and sophisticated technology which can generally

TABLE 5.7.   Distribution Pattern of Technology Licensing from Japan and the United States in Korean Manufacturing Industries I: 1962–February 28, 1993

Technology Licensing from Japan
cases (%)

Industries	Low-Technology	High-Technology	Subtotal
Labor-Intensive	156 (4%)	1,424 (37%)	1,580 (41%)
Capital-Intensive	391 (10%)	1,910 (49%)	2,301 (59%)
Subtotal	547 (14%)	3,334 (86%)	3,881 (100%)

(**Note:** Others are 203, therefore, the total is 4,084)

Technology Licensing from the United States
cases (%)

Industries	Low-Technology	High-Technology	Subtotal
Labor-Intensive	125 (6%)	486 (24%)	611 (30%)
Capital-Intensive	132 (7%)	1,297 (63%)	1,429 (70%)
Subtotal	257 (13%)	1,783 (87%)	2,040 (100%)

(**Note:** Others are 139, therefore, the total is 2,179)

be characterized as capital-intensive, whereas Japan tends to transfer mature and standardized technology which is mostly labor-intensive. Examining the nature of these patterns helps to illustrate how host-country policies can influence the composition of technology transfer from donor states.

Again, the figures in Table 5.7, which are cumulative cases for the 1962–February 28, 1993, period, do not inform us whether or not there is any change in the type of TL relating to industrial and economic conditions and government policy over TL of that period. Therefore, we analyze the TL distribution pattern from Japan and the United States for the 1962–1972, the 1973–1978, and subsequent subperiods. As indicated in Table 5.8, TL from Japan and the United States are clearly concentrated in the high-technology industries during the entire period. Again, these results reflect the rapid transformation of Korean industrialization and thereby an increasing demand for high technologies. When compared to the priorities of the various five-year plans, these results reflect the government's emphasis increasingly placed on acquiring more high technologies (Hahm, Plein, and Florida 1994; Kim and Dahlman 1992; Yu 1986). Such patterns stand in sharp contrast with Kojima's (1977) analysis.

TECHNOLOGY TRANSFER AND THE DEVELOPMENTAL STATE

By analyzing Korean technology-transfer policy experiences from 1962 to 1993, specifically two transfer practices, direct investment and technology-licensing patterns from the United States and Japan to Korean manufacturing industries, we offer a new perspective on the dynamics of international technology transfer in newly industrialized countries such as Korea. The prevailing view in much of the dependence and the neoclassical literature on international technology transfer from developed countries to developing countries has focused on the strong position of the former and the weak position of the latter. In sharp contrast to this viewpoint, but consistent with the developmental state perspective, we find that the pattern and character of direct investment and technology licensing has been shaped, in large part, by technology-transfer policy strategies advanced and implemented by the Korean government. This finding is supported, in part, by analysis that reveals no substantial difference between Korea's principal sources of technology transfer—the United States and Japan—in distribution patterns of two transfer practices in Korean manufacturing industries. Contrasting with previous studies, these empirical findings suggest that a host country's policy toward technology transfer can be a powerful determinant in patterns of technology transfer.

By analyzing shifts in government technology policy and their impacts on the sectoral composition of direct investment and technology licensings in terms of both case and dollar value,

TABLE 5.8.   Distribution Pattern of Technology Licensing from Japan and the United States in Korean Manufacturing Industries II: 1962–February 28, 1993

From Japan
cases (%)

Period	Low-Technology	High-Technology	Subtotal
1962–1972	29	186	215
	(13%)	(87%)	(100%)
1973–1978	80	379	459
	(17%)	(83%)	(100%)
1979–Feb 28, 1993	438	2,769	3,207
	(14%)	(86%)	(100%)
1962–Feb 28, 1993	547	3,334	3,881
	(14%)	(86%)	(100%)

From the United States
cases (%)

Period	Low-Technology	High-Technology	Subtotal
1962–1972	18	52	70
	(26%)	(74%)	(100%)
1973–1978	32	130	162
	(20%)	(80%)	(100%)
1979–Feb 28, 1993	207	1,601	1,808
	(11%)	(89%)	(100%)
1962–Feb 28, 1993	257	1,783	2,040
	(13%)	(87%)	(100%)

we find strong influence of government policy on the sectoral composition of direct investments and technology licensing. The overall trends of sectoral composition of direct investments and technology licensing reflect the structural transformation of the Korean economy and government policy which placed emphasis on increasing the acquisition of more sophisticated technologies as development progressed. Second, by comparing technologies transferred from the United States and Japan to Korean manufacturing industries in terms of the level of technological sophistication and production factor intensity, we find no significant difference in the distribution patterns of direct investments and technology licensing from the United States and Japan. Direct investment and technology licensing involving sources from both countries concentrate in the capital-intensive, high-technology industries. Indeed, since the early 1970s when Korea entered its growth stage in industrialization, there has been a steady trend in the distribution pattern of both direct investments and TL from the United States and Japan toward high-technology applications. This pattern suggests that Korean government policy has played a role in shaping patterns of technology transfer.

Our findings are best understood in the context of broad policy goals set out by the government in its Five-Year Economic and Social Development Plans that have been implemented since 1962. The objective of the early plans was to encourage the take-off of the transformation of the Korean economy from an agrarian to an industrial base. The government utilized such policy tools as liberal direct-investment arrangements to encourage the inflow of established manufacturing processes. The presence of an inexpensive and well-motivated work force no doubt provided an incentive for such investments by foreign sources.

In the early 1970s the transformation of the Korean economy became apparent. In response, the government shifted its emphasis to sustaining growth through policies designed to establish an industrial base where domestic rather than foreign players prevailed. Notable changes in technology-transfer policy strategy included encouraging technology-licensing arrangements in order to acquire more sophisticated production resources and tempering foreign dominance through joint venture requirements. As the 1980s progressed, Korea continued to liberalize direct-investment and technology-licensing arrangements to encourage further development of the capital-intensive, high-technology industries.

In short, a case can be made for the influence of the host-state government over economic activity. The greater the ability of the host country to exert control over the economy, the better position it is in to influence technology-transfer patterns. The strong Korean state of the 1960s to 1980s allowed considerable influence through direct-investment and technology-licensing policy schemes. It will be interesting to see how influential Korean policy will be in the future as the state disengages from such practices as control of lending institutions and determining which industries and technologies will have priority through chaebol arrangements. But recent general downward trends in direct investment raise possible implications that invite special consideration on the limits of Korea's discretion in shaping patterns of technology transfer.

Apart from the host country's policy strategies, two other factors come into play in shaping the nature of technology transfer. First, the domestic capacity to attract and assimilate new technologies needs to be considered. A host country's ability to attract foreign investment and the capability to incorporate new technologies is dependent upon the host country's resource base. For example, early in its industrialization takeoff period, Korean capacity was limited to relatively low-level and labor-intensive technologies and practices. With recent rising wage rates, increasingly negative attitudes toward manual labor, the erosion of the traditional work ethic, and the growing cost of capital, Korea has lost some of its attractiveness as a site for foreign investment.

The second factor is the willingness of foreign donor interests to engage in technology transfer with the host state. Technology transfer is an exchange relationship. The host country must be able to offer advantages, either tacit or expressed, to attract foreign investment. Changes in technology and policy can alter this relationship. For example, the emergence of knowledge-intensive industries (such as computer software and biotechnology) has seen a growing reluctance among potential donors interested in entering into technology-transfer arrangements. There is concern that such arrangements will lead to a quick appropriation of the technology by the host country—leading to a situation where competition might emerge.

The advent of new, knowledge-intensive technologies since the late 1980s has forced Korea to reconsider its technology-transfer strategies. Having achieved a standard of industrial sophistication, the acquisition of knowledge, processes, techniques, and skills rather than the machinery of production is the driving force in contemporary technology-transfer policy. However, in a highly competitive global marketplace, high-technology leaders are not as willing to license new technologies (see the yearly data of tech-nology licensing in Table 5.9A). In short, today's nascent entrants into high-technology markets are seen as tomorrow's fierce com-petitors. As a result, Korea is now entertaining direct investment as a means of attracting such new technologies as genetic engi-neering, semiconductors, and telecommunications. Given Korea's limited capacity to create generic high technologies and to develop new products and markets, following the U.S. focus on "breakthrough" technology clearly remains unrealistic in most cases, with the possible exception of semiconductor memory prod-ucts. In this regard technology transfer, particularly direct invest-ment, could open up a more realistic perspective of gradually building up new capabilities for technology innovations (Ernst 1994). Therefore, as a premium is increasingly being placed on technological sophistication as a key to international competitive-ness, the role of the state in shaping patterns of technology trans-fer, particularly direct investment, becomes a critical element in economic policy planning.

Of particular interest in this regard is a possible future role of direct investment as a vehicle for technological development. Technology-licensing arrangements lose their luster when those in possession of leading-edge technologies perceive the risk of losing advantages through knowledge-sharing arrangements. Access to this type of knowledge cannot be gained through restrictive gov-ernment policy over direct investment. Participation in technol-ogy cooperation networks with foreign firms is the only alternative. Here, outdated policy instruments would seem to have been an important constraint. Recent moves to streamline foreign investment regulations are not very convincing. Indeed, as we noted earlier and Table 5.9B indicates, the yearly data illustrate a substantial decline of direct investments in terms of both cases and values in the manufacturing sector, particularly after 1987. As a result, Korea today has one of the lowest rates of inward direct investment in East Asia—despite serious policy efforts to bring direct investments back into the country as a vehicle for acceler-ated technology diffusion (Ernst 1994). In 1992, for instance, Korea experienced an overall decline of direct investment of 36 percent to a low of $501 million and a decline in the manufactur-ing sector of 40 percent to $422 million. Through a series of gov-ernment-led initiatives, Korea sought to relax foreign direct-investment restrictions throughout much of the early 1990s. By

TABLE 5.9A.   Total Technology Licensing 1987–1993

	Cases	$1,000
1987	637	523,706.6
1988	751	676,365.6
1989	763	888,573.0
1990	738	1,086,990.1
1991	582	1,183,786.9
1992	533	850,632.9
1993	707	945,900.0

(**Source:** Korean Ministry of Finance & Economy, "Trends in Technology Inducement," Seoul, 1994)

In 1994 the Economic Planning Board (EPB) and the Ministry of Finance (MOF) merged to become the Ministry of Finance and Economy (MFE). Prior to this time, the EPB was responsible for government reporting for direct investment while the MOF was responsible for reports on technology licensing. With the establishment of the MFE, these responsibilities were combined.

1996, the level of investment reached $3.20 billion. This represents an increase of 64 percent from 1995 levels, an increase of 144 percent from 1994 levels, and an increase of 258 percent from 1992 levels (Ministry of Finance and Economy 1997). Nevertheless, Korea still lags behind other East Asian countries in levels of foreign direct investment.

Under current circumstances, the very same features of government technology-transfer policy that until the late 1980s were conducive for the rapid expansion of Korea's export-led industrialization have now become constraints for attempts to sustain Korean industrialization through an upgrading of its technological capability using a direct-investment arrangement. The case of Korea in the early 1990s is particularly illustrative. Preferring a regime of technology-licensing arrangements, the Korean government was forced to reconsider its position in the face of new technological realities. With the emergence of knowledge-intensive high-technology practices and processes, which represented considerable research and development investment and proprietary interests, those in possession of such new technologies were not as willing to engage in technology-licensing arrangements. Instead, in order to protect their investments, these interests prefer

TABLE 5.9B.   Total Direct Investment 1987–1994 (cases/$1,000)

	Agriculture, Fisheries, and Mining	Manufacturing	Service	Total
1987	5 (3,709)	321 (772,602)	36 (287,016)	362 (1,063,327)
1988	4 (11,493)	272 (736,189)	66 (535,050)	342 (1,282,732)
1989	1 (3,475)	194 (747,433)	141 (359,371)	336 (1,090,279)
1990	1 (526)	135 (583,313)	159 (218,693)	295 (802,532)
1991	0 (1,172)	107 (1,069,286)	178 (325,638)	287 (1,396,096)
1992	1 (2,197)	81 (647,012)	152 (245,394)	234 (894,603)
1993	1 (127)	80 (526,817)	192 (517,330)	273 (1,044,274)
1994	1 (270)	136 (401,693)	277 (914,542)	414 (1,316,505)
1995	0	380 (884,104)	492 (1,056,896)	872 (1,941,000)
1996	0	369 (1,930,000)	597 (1,271,000)	966 (3,201,000)

(**Source:** Korean Ministry of Finance & Economy, "The Current State of Foreign Investment," Seoul, 1997)

to engage in direct-investment practices. In order to gain new technologies, Korea has been forced to alter its stance on direct investment. Therefore, since different stages in industrial and technological evolution call for a different set of technology-transfer policies, it is imperative to analyze technology transfer from a dynamic perspective of the developing state in transition.

The Korean experience may be seen as a highly illustrative case in point regarding the ability to control the flow of foreign direct investment and technology licensing. As we have detailed, it also displays the limits of state influence. The Korean experience is not unlike those of other newly industrialized countries (NICs) in controlling inflows of investment and technology for the purposes of state-directed economic development policy objectives. However, the distinctive character of other states, brought about by the convergence of history, culture, and resource endowments, invite both comparison and contrast. In particular, the Korean experience invites discussion in the context of other East Asian NICs. Since most tend to be hailed as successes, interest obviously turns on similarities and contrasts. But a comparative dimension invites discussion in association with the fortunes of other NICs, as well.

Among Asia's NICs, Korea and Taiwan stand at the apex of success. For this reason, comparative analysis often focuses on the two (see D. Kang 1995). There are important similarities and distinctions between the Korean and Taiwanese experiences. Perhaps the most important similarity deals with both states' use of direct investment and technology licensing as tools for economic development. Taiwan's regulation of direct investment and technology licensing has some parallels to the Korean experience. During Taiwan's initial industrialization phase from the late 1950s through the early 1970s, direct investment became a key force in developing a manufacturing base (World Bank 1993:132–33). Since this time, greater emphasis has been placed on restricting direct investment and encouraging technology-licensing arrangements—though not to the extent seen in Korea (World Bank 1993:21). Like Korea, Taiwan has recently embarked on initiatives to develop its high-technology base. We might expect Taiwan to feel the same pressures to allow direct investment as Korea has when facing these knowledge-sensitive technologies.

But there are important contrasts between Taiwan and Korea, as well. One of the most distinctive differences relates to firm ownership patterns in the two countries. A critical dimension to state control of technology and capital inflows in Taiwan stems from the nature of firm ownership. Among NICs, in general, Taiwan is characterized by a greater than average level of state ownership of enterprises. The contrast is particularly stark in comparison with Korea, where direct state ownership of firms has been very limited (D. Kang 1995:569). Further, among privately held companies in Taiwan, there has been a tendency toward rather small-scale family-oriented firms (see World Bank 1993:161; D. Kang 1995; Fallows 1994). This, too, stands in contrast with the *chaebol*, or business conglomerate, which dominates Korean economy.

The emphasis on mixing direct investment and technology licensing in Korea and Taiwan stands in contrast with other NICs in East Asia. Hong Kong and Singapore have encouraged direct investment as the primary tool for industrialization (World Bank 1993:21). Other newly industrializing states in Asia, such as Indonesia, Malaysia, and Thailand, have followed suit. Fallows (1994: 263–69) warns that the most recently developing East Asian countries, such as the Philippines, Malaysia, and Thailand, by allowing direct investment, have exposed themselves to external dominance, especially by Japan. Bernard and Ravenhill (1995) observe a growing trend in which Japan, and to a lesser extent Korea and Taiwan, are utilizing developing Asian economies as a platform for export-based production. In these trade triangles, developed Northeast Asian states supply technologies and manufacturing arrangements to developing countries, which in turn export finished products to the United States, Western Europe, and other foreign markets. Because these arrangements are set up through direct-investment schemes, profits flow back to those providing the means of manufacture and technology.

The economic and political desirability of such arrangements is subject to interpretation. Bernard and Ravenhill (1995) warn that such arrangements may lead to regional tensions, primarily between Asian NICs and Japan. In addition, they warn that the United States faces stiff competition from such arrangements. This point is echoed by others as well (see Fallows 1994). On the other hand, adherents of the neoclassical approach to economic development (see for example, World Bank 1993; Krueger 1995), tend to look favorably on direct investment in developing states. Such arrangements are seen as providing the spark for broader development, since foreign investment provides a multiplier effect that creates support services and industries.

In general, in the case of East Asia, both host states and foreign sources have been attracted to direct investment not so much to develop domestic markets in the host states, but as an export platform (World Bank 1993:318). This helps to explain the recent movement of more developed East Asian states into direct-investment arrangements with East Asian developing countries. Thus, for example, Japan and Taiwan have made substantial foreign direct-investment arrangements in Malaysia to take advantage of relatively low wage rates (World Bank 1993:302). Korea has expanded its involvement in direct investment as well, with the pace of investments greatly accelerating during the 1980s (Bernard and Ravenhill 1995:182).

Ultimately, the ability of NICs to draw lessons from the successes and failures of more economically and technologically advanced states is a critical tool in achieving economic and societal objectives. The World Bank, known for its neoclassical views, acknowledges that government intervention in Northeast Asia "resulted in higher and more equal growth than otherwise would have occurred" but observes that similar efforts in developing countries elsewhere have not been successful (World Bank 1993:6). But the World Bank suggests that the experiences of Southeast Asian economies, which saw minimal government intervention, may be a better model of development (World Bank 1993:7). Perhaps the World Bank is correct in asserting that the Korean model may not be entirely replicable elsewhere. But this begs a larger question. For what the Korean experience illustrates is that a developmental state, even in the earlier stages of industrialization, has the ability to shape the flow and content of foreign technologies. Assuming that the state has the capacity to influence the actions of domestic capital actors, which is admittedly a significant assumption, a mix of policy tools presents an important resource in economic development and planning.

TECHNOLOGY TRANSFER IN THE POSTDEVELOPMENTAL STATE

As we noted in chapters 2 and 4, we have begun to distinguish technology policy as a component of industrial development policy schemes. As argued by Branscomb (1991), through technology policy government pursues courses of action which facilitate technological innovation and foster its access by sectoral interests. Therefore, the growing importance of technology policy for international competitiveness cannot be overemphasized. Technology transfer, technological advance, and industrial application are now seen as key components in an overall economic and industrial policy strategy in Korea. This emphasis is characteristic of highly industrialized nations as well (see Graham 1992; Skolnikoff 1993). And yet the increase and intensity of international market factors in domestic affairs, from both a societal and policy perspective, raises questions regarding the ability of the state to determine desired policy goals and influence technology-transfer patterns and outcomes. Indeed, it is in the area of technology transfer that the challenges posed to the postdevelopmental state are well illuminated.

From a political perspective, the ability to dictate the flow of technology transfer will be diminished by the emergence of other institutional actors voicing policy preferences which might challenge those of the executive. We can expect that to occur if the Korean legislature matures into an institution which can serve as a vehicle for representing and articulating group and sectoral interests. Different societal interests may have competing priorities and agendas as to what is best for Korea. For example, an increasingly environmentally conscious populace may express an unwillingness to attract those technologies which pose an environmental threat. This has certainly been the case in postindustrial or postmaterial societies, where risk consciousness and quality of life issues have gained prominent places on the national stage (see Bell 1973; Inglehart 1977; Douglas and Wildavsky 1982).

If one of the hallmarks of the postdeveloped state is the emergence of socially conscious voices in the populace, another is a preoccupation with preserving a sense of self-reliance and independence in the global stage. In the case of Korean technology-transfer policies, this may be manifested in resistance to foreign direct-investment practices. Some might rebel at the idea of encouraging foreign direct investment, no matter how necessary it might be, because it is a symbol, and perhaps source, of foreign influence, if not domination. And yet necessity has dictated that the Korean government change policy course and encourage foreign direct investment in order to participate in high-technology markets. The consequence of this is to further diminish the influence of the state over economic and trade matters.

One of the demands of government in the postdevelopmental state, ideally, is to provide a venue and process for differences of opinion, interest, and policy prescription to be aired, deliberated, and ironed out. This would have been an alien concept for the authoritarian arrangements of the Korean developmental state, where the practice was to impose the will of those in executive power. Now, as we have outlined in the previous chapter, the role of the executive will increasingly focus on his broker abilities in remedying conflict and constructing policy coalitions.

We believe that the balance of policy influence in Korea's transitionary institutional arrangements will gravitate toward the bureaucracy. Technology transfer has played a key role in Korea's developmental experience—and the successes of these efforts can in large part be claimed by the bureaucracy. Indeed, given the disjunctive change in the Korean presidency, the institutional memory of technology transfer rests firmly in the hands of the bureaucracy. Given this situation, we can expect the bureaucracy to exert greater sway over technology-transfer policy. We can expect the presidency to become particularly dependent on the bureaucracy for policy advice. However, an increase in standing relative to other institutions will not necessarily translate into influence outside of government.

Perhaps the most central conditions associated with the emergence of the postdevelopmental state are economic changes in Korea, which are calling into question the ability of the state to influence the course of technology acquisition, transfer, and adoption. The control of technology transfer has been an important instrument in the Korean state's efforts to shape the course of industrialization and economic development. Given the transnational nature of international firms and trade arrangements, the actions taken by individual firms and their various foreign subsidiaries may overshadow the policy actions taken by a state. The postdevelopmental state must also face the pressures exerted by international organizations and arrangements. The intricate web that links trade, industrialization, and capital access in the global arena may limit the influence of the state. For example, it is clear that some bodies, such as the World Bank, prefer host countries to have policies which facilitate foreign direct investment (see World Bank 1993). In the postdevelopmental state, the bureaucracy may be relied on more to study and explain conditions than to assist in the formulation and take the lead in implementing technology-transfer policy. The state's ability to exert control over technology transfer, as a whole, has declined in recent years. The combination of global trade and policy factors coupled with the changing nature of technology has diminished the influence of executive and bureaucratic efforts to regulate the flow and character of technology transfer.

CONCLUSION

The prevailing view in much of the dependence and the neoclassical literature on international technology transfer from developed countries to developing countries has focused on the strong position of the former and the weak position of the latter. Under this view, developing countries that receive technologies from abroad are perceived as dependent on the wishes and whims of more powerful donors (see, for example, Dunning 1988; Kojima 1973, 1977, 1978, 1985; Mason 1980; Ozawa 1979; Roemer 1975, 1976). Our findings stand in contrast to this viewpoint. Consistent with the developmental state perspective, we find that a host country's policy toward technology transfer can be an important factor in patterns of transfer, at least in the Korean experience.

We believe that our findings have broader implications for the literature, because they challenge some of the basic assumptions of neoclassical and dependency theory and reinforce emerging frameworks that speak to the importance of state policies as a determinant of the course of development. While we do not discount the importance of exogenous factors as influences in patterns of technology transfer—consider, for example Korea's new posture toward direct investment, given recent advances in knowledge-intensive technologies—we stress that the policies of host states should be given further attention in the study of the developmental experience. Conceptually, it would be tempting to develop a counterfactual argument to separate out policy impacts by positing what the effects would be without policy intervention. However, construction of such models are rife with challenges, considering such factors as historical forces, effects of time, and perspective of study (see Jones and Sakong 1980; Johnson 1982).

The Korean experience reveals how the state can use various policy tools to shape patterns of technology transfer through direct investment and technology licensing; patterns of technology transfer cannot be explained simply by concentrating on what has been transferred from donor countries such as the United States and Japan. Rather, we need to turn our focus to the host country and what policy strategies have been adopted to shape patterns of technology transfer. In short, the question turns from the economics of what to the policies of how technology transfer is accomplished. We argue that knowledge of policy options and possibilities in the area of technology transfer becomes an important aspect in understanding a country's economic and industrial planning. Also critical to our understanding of technology transfer is how technology and market conditions, as well as the desires of policy makers, shape the contours of policy influence.

NOTES

1. This chapter draws, in part, on earlier research published as Hahm, Plein, and Florida (1994).

2. In contrast to Lee (1984), E. Kim (1992) argues that there have been differences in the pattern of direct investment from the United States and Japan to Korea. In particular, U.S. direct investment tends to concentrate on the manufacturing sector, while Japanese direct investment focuses on the service sector, especially hotels. However, the difference between the perspectives of Lee and Kim is that the former concentrates on manufacturing while the latter combines sectors for analysis. In our analysis, we focus on the pattern of investment regarding manufacturing. We do this because we are concerned with technological development in Korea. Obviously, manufacturing-related investment is an engine of technological development.

3. For further detail on legal and bureaucratic control mechanisms and objectives of changes of policy over direct investments, see Cho 1985; Mardon 1990; Yu 1986.

4. Other factors contributed to the decline of direct investment as well. For example, the emphasis the government placed on foreign firms contributing to local value-added activities and the priority placed on technology transfer to enhance Korea's own technological capacity proved to be a disincentive to foreign involvement. Japanese firms were particularly reluctant to divulge manufacturing and production processes, fearing involuntary technology leakages. The growing competitive position of Korean firms also created disincentives to foreign investors. Rather than compete with Korean producers, both American and Japanese firms decided to shift operations to lower wage areas elsewhere in East Asia (see Ernst 1994). Interestingly, by the early 1990s, Korean firms had also become direct investors in low-wage East Asian states (Bernard and Ravenhill 1995:182).

5. In this regard, Kim and Dahlman (1992), Haggard (1990), Mardon (1990), and Pack and Westphal (1986) argue that direct investment has played a minor role in Korean development and has certainly been much less important than in other developing countries because Korea emphasized external borrowing rather than direct investment. Moreover, direct

investment participation was rejected in the sectors deemed strategic and sensitive through government intervention.

6. The figures in the third column of Table 5.1, which are cumulative cases and values for the 1982–1993.1 period, do not inform us whether or not there is any rapid recent change in the patterns of direct investment.

7. Table 5.2A has a greater total because each case is assigned to participant donor countries. In many cases, more than one country will be participating in a particular direct-investment venture.

8. These ceilings stipulated that royalties should be set within 3 percent of sales, and that contract duration would not exceed three years for licenses in the manufacturing sector (see Yu 1986 for details).

9. Tables 5.4A and 5.4B also reveal an interesting dimension in the pattern of TL arrangements between Korean firms and Japan and the United States. As Tables 5.4A and 5.4B indicate, while the total number of TLs from the United States is smaller than that from Japan, the total amount of the royalty payments is larger for the United States than for Japan. The average for TL royalty payments to the United States is $1.57 million, whereas the average for TL royalty payments to Japan is $0.54 million. However, we cannot assume from this that the TLs from the United States reflect a higher degree of technological sophistication. Many other factors affect these differences, such as geographical distance and cultural differences. As we discuss later, we also cannot precisely examine the difference of technological sophistication of TL from the United States and Japan in terms of royalty payments because of limited data availability.

10. More specifically, from 1961 through 1966, the First FYESDP, the annual average of TL amounted to only 7 cases per year. But it dramatically increased to 57 during the Second FYESDP of 1967–1971, to 87 during the 1972–1976 Third FYESDP period, to 245 during the 1977–1981 Fourth FYESDP period, to 416 during the 1982–1986 Fifth FYESDP period, and during the 1987–1991 Sixth FYESDP period it rose to about 694 cases per year.

11. Our analysis of the distribution pattern of direct investment and TL is primarily based on the number of cases rather than the value or the royalty payment. Because the Korean government does not report data for the value of direct investment and TL royalty payments for specific countries, time periods, and economic sectors, we are unable to compare U.S. and Japanese involvement in specific sectors for the specified time periods.

12. Measurements focusing on direct investments and TL only capture a portion of the overall activity involved in technology transfer. Other measures are technical collaboration through training and education, import of embodied technology-intensive goods, etc. (see Kim and Dahlman 1992; Pack and Westphal 1986).

13. We classify industries into the four industry groups in accordance with level of technological sophistication and production factor intensity

(labor/capital requirement ratio). These are: labor-intensive, low-technology industries; labor-intensive, high-technology industries; capital-intensive, low-technology industries; and capital-intensive, high-technology industries. Following Lee (1984), we used Hufbauer's (1970) estimates of factor and skill intensities of goods.

The labor-intensive, low-technology industries are food, tobacco, textiles, wearing apparel, leather and leather products, footwear, wood and wood cork products, furniture and fixtures, rubber products, plastic products, fabricated metal products (except machinery and equipment), and other manufacturing. The labor-intensive, high-technology industries are printing, publishing and allied industries, machinery, electrical machinery, apparatus, appliances and supplies, transport equipment, and professional and scientific equipment. The capital-intensive, low-technology industries are beverages, paper and paper products, pottery, china and earthenware, glass and glass products, other nonmetallic mineral products, and basic iron and steel products. The capital-intensive, high-technology industries are industrial chemicals, other chemical products, petroleum products, and basic nonferrous metal products.

14. Our analysis is based on the number of cases rather than the dollar value of the direct investment and the royalty payment of the technology licensing. Without looking at the dollar value, it is difficult to know what to make of the convergence cited in Japanese and U.S. practices. The number of cases could converge without the values converging. For instance, Japanese firms accounted for well over twice as many cases of direct investment but only one-third greater value of direct investment than U.S. firms. Similarly, U.S. companies accounted for roughly half as many licenses as Japanese companies but over 1.5 times greater value (as measured by licensing fees paid). Together, these numbers suggest, contrary to what we conclude, that U.S. companies were transferring different and more valuable technology than Japanese firms. To respond to this concern, we have tried to clarify the limitations of our data. Our data cannot examine the patterns of direct investment from the United States and Japan in terms of dollar value in a specific time period by economic sector because of limited data availability. Our data also cannot examine the patterns of technology licensing from the United States and Japan in terms of royalty payments in a specific time period by economic sector. We strongly believe that no government data of other countries allows for this. With these constraints, we have tried to show the total number of cases and dollar amounts of direct investments and technology licensing by economic sector through only three specific time periods (see Tables 5.1 and 5.3). With this attempt, we can see more clearly the effect of government policy on the sectoral composition of direct investments and technology licensing. The conclusions of these specific sectoral composition analyses of direct investment and technology licensing are consistent with those of our analysis, based on four industrial classifications. We have tried to analyze direct investment from the United States and Japan

to Korean manufacturing industries in term of values, but only the period of 1962 to 1993.1 with four industrial classifications (see Table 5.3B). We find that there is no substantial difference between the United States and Japan. Both countries' direct investments in terms of value concentrate on capital-intensive, high-technology-intensive industry.

15. However, when investments are divided only between the labor-intensive and the capital-intensive industries, Japanese direct investments are somewhat more concentrated in the labor-intensive industries than U.S. direct investments. As argued by Dunning (1988), Mason (1980), and Lee (1984), this difference may reflect the difference between production factor endowments of the two countries. In the case of Japan up until the late 1970s, labor-intensive practices characterized various manufacturing industrial sectors, whereas U.S. manufacturing is characterized by capital-intensive practices (see Yoon 1990).

16. Although direct investment of both countries was highly concentrated in the high-technology industries, U.S. patterns were slightly more concentrated than Japan in the capital-intensive, high-technology industries.

17. This finding is comparable to Chou's (1988) analysis of the Taiwanese experience.

6

Conclusion

The investigation of transition and change in Korea has been somewhat popular in recent years (see, for example, Amsden 1989; Haggard and Moon 1990; Koo 1993a; E. Kim 1993; Haggard and Kaufman 1995; Casper and Taylor 1996). Useful as these studies have been, we have sought to distinguish our work by providing a more substantial theoretical underpinning to examine change in executive–bureaucratic arrangements and by revisiting and critiquing some of the interpretations offered for the root causes of regime change in the Korean experience. Previous efforts to interpret the Korean experience have often been descriptive in nature and, almost as a rule, have concentrated on the broad contours of social and institutional change. We have sought to provide a more interpretive and focused evaluation which concentrates on the dynamics of executive–bureaucratic relationships since the imposition of rigid authoritarian rule in 1961 through recent reforms in the Korean system under the tutelage of President Kim Young Sam.

Since the early 1960s, the Korean government has taken an active role in the country's impressive economic and industrial development. But this development was bought at the price of the initiation and continuation of the strong authoritarian state. Indeed, the legitimacy of the military regimes that seized and maintained the reins of power depended on economic growth as a means of legitimizing their hold on power. However, the strong authoritarian state that produced rapid growth also planted the seeds for its decline. Two important by-products of economic development, namely social and political democratization and economic liberalization and globalization, appear to have hastened the developmental state's declining ability to influence Korean society and economy. Korea is now in the midst of social and political democratic transition and economic and industrial restructuring. These forces have given rise to trade unionism, greater economic independence of large corporations and business conglomerates, and the emergence of a more activist press and the expression of popular criticism and concern for government policies.

At the same time, big business interests have enjoyed greater independence with the retreat of government from investment and credit control. The authoritarian executive–bureaucratic nexus has faced not only mounting social pressure from capital and labor, but other factors as well. One factor has been growing internal tensions and contradictions within the state between presidential regimes and the bureaucracy. Another factor focuses on the growing internationalization of Korea's economic sphere. By implication, the consequences of past policy success in economic development grew to threaten the stability of strong-state arrangements (Evans 1995; Koo 1993b). Moreover, there is ample evidence that the authoritarian executive–bureaucratic nexus is no longer an effective agent in shaping the course of economic development.

Additionally, rapid economic progress has also brought new realities to the authoritarian structure of the Korean presidency and bureaucracy and their nexus. New presidential arrangements characterized by such factors as limited and fixed terms as well as institutional and constitutional accountability have diminished the absolute influence of the president over the bureaucracy. The bureaucracy may be more independent in institutional terms, but its ability to hold sway over other social and business actors through policy control is limited and perhaps diminishing. Such conditions may lead to bureaucratic fragmentation and conflict. Under these conditions, the effectiveness of the bureaucracy as an instrument for policy development and implementation diminishes. As a result, executive and bureaucratic activity may come to be perceived as a drag on effective industrial and economic development. Nevertheless, though presidential and bureaucratic influence over social and economic matters has decreased, both institutions will remain central actors in Korean politics and policy. Though the forces of social and economic liberalization are shaping changes in contemporary Korea, the authoritarian tradition is deeply embedded in this nation.

CONTOURS OF THE DEVELOPMENTAL STATE IN TRANSITION

Observers of state development may do well to examine experiences of states in the face of what we might call postdevelopmentalism. As we outlined in chapter 2, the postdevelopmental state is characterized by a breakdown in the influence that authoritarian–executive arrangements once enjoyed over society, economy, and, indeed, other institutional branches of government. Because of the power of economic growth, influence over the market becomes diminished. Because of symbolic and substantive political reforms, the power of public opinion and electoral action has strengthened. Because of governmental reorganization, power concentrated in the executive erodes as policy influence and responsibility is atomized among nascent political institutions, such as legislatures, courts, and local governments.

Our analysis suggests that significant structural changes are fundamentally altering the composition of the Korean state and its relationship to societal and economic actors. The most general sketch of change in Korea illustrates two startling transformations. One is the decline of authoritarian arrangements whereby presidents have held undisputed control over the levers of policy and related economic developments. These changes stem from both structural conditions and calculated decisions made by political actors. Thus, desperate concessions made to capital interests in the waning years of authoritarian control; societal pressures for greater accountability; the strengthening of bureaucratic influence; and the emergence of the courts, legislature, and local governments have all contributed to this change. The other change is the diminishing influence of the state over economic affairs. The resources and the influence of economic actors, especially in the aggregate, as manifested in market behavior, have outstripped the capacity of the state to control economic development. This loss of influence has been compounded by other factors as well, including technological developments which have made established policy controls on foreign direct investment less tenable and the pressures brought upon the state from foreign actors who seek concessions and agreements as part of new global market activity and regulation.

If Korea can stand as an illustrative experience of the newly industrialized country, which we argue it does, then we can tender a number of generalizations about the developmental state in transition. First, developmental state governments are more complex than is often portrayed. The state is not a monolith, but a complex network of actors with different bases of power and authority. In Korea, the main power axis has fallen on a line anchored by the presidency and the bureaucracy. Failure to see distinctions within the state led to depictions of the experiences of developmental–authoritarian states, such as Korea, that have tended to stress the strong, determined role of the state. Such characterizations give a flavor of determined and concerted efforts that are the product of rigid hierarchies and strong bureaucratic compliance to policy directives. But by moving beyond the veil from which we have defined the state, we can see how the internal tensions, relationships, and arrangements within the state display insights on the developmental–authoritarian state experience. In the Korean experience, by decoupling the president and his inner circle from administrative arrangements, we can note the internal tensions that make up the dynamics of executive–bureaucratic relationships.

Second, contemporary accounts of the Korean developmental experience tend to overlook the dynamic role of the state in its influence over the course of development. The power of the state is not a constant but fluctuates. Because of a failure to appreciably recognize this, some accounts (see Haggard and Moon 1990; E. Kim 1993) portray the state as redirecting the economy through new priorities and policies (e.g., the move away from *chaebol* support in the 1980s and the corresponding emphasis on small- and mid-size firm development). If one holds the power of the state to be constant, then the new policy orientation appears to be an independent action taken by the state. But in Korea this is not the case. The Korean state has lost its ability to control economic development. Policy changes in the 1980s were not a reflection of reprioritization under some grand design. Instead they are an indication of the marginalization of the state in a time of rapid economic expansion, as a result of prior concessions to capital interests that were made during the Chun regime.

Third, both structural factors and individual policy elite choices have contributed to the marginalization of the Korean state. Social and economic conditions provided the factors needed for change. Faced with challenges, authoritarian policy elites chose short-term response strategies which undermined their own longer-term interests. The actions taken by the Chun regime are a clear example of how short-term political objectives may be bought at the expense of long-term interests. While the outcome, from a social and democratic perspective, has been beneficial for the Korean people, at least for the near term, the concessions made to well-entrenched capital interests sowed the seeds for the authoritarian state's demise. Once the state began to cede control over investment and finance, the influence of the government diminished.

Fourth, it was the marginalization of the state in economic matters, and not the democracy movement per se, that provided the main leverage for a fundamental shift in the nature of Korean politics, both during and at the close of the Roh regime. For those who embrace the tenets and promise of democracy, there is a temptation to laud credit for Korea's social liberalization on those agitating for political reform. There is no doubt that decades of protest and resistance against the authoritarian state were important in Korea's transformation (for discussions, see Han 1989; E. Kim 1994; Lee 1994; Koo 1993b). But we emphasize that concessions made to capital interests were the trigger for liberalization. The consequence of this is obvious. Institutional change has not been undertaken to accommodate democratic and popular movements so much as it has been a reflection of pressures exerted by more elite, that is capital, interest.

Fifth, much of the recent commentary on change in Korea has been too sanguine about democratic development. There are many obstacles to successful democratization which can be described by the structural–rational model. Furthermore, distinctions between political and social democratization and economic liberalization are often confused or overlooked in discussions of developmental state and modernization experiences. We seek to decouple these two important elements in our examination of the Korean case. Korea faces troubling prospects, reasons for which are rooted in past and present circumstances. The lack of a tradition for compromise and loyal opposition in politics means that Korea's nascent party system is built on the thinnest of reeds. In addition, the power of capital interests is still substantial in Korea, meaning that there may still be cause for labor turmoil and other manifestations of popular resentment against concentrated wealth and policies that are seen as too accommodating to these interests.[1] In short, the future role of the state is uncertain.

THE CHALLENGE OF INSTITUTIONAL DEVELOPMENT: THE TRANSFORMATION OF THE KOREAN PRESIDENCY AND BUREAUCRACY

Under strong authoritarian state arrangements, the Korean president has traditionally been the central actor in state action. Through the force of personality and the support of a close-knit team of advisors, from the early 1960s until the early 1990s Korean presidents held primacy over policy deliberation, planning, and implementation. As has been noted by many observers (see E. Kim 1994; Haggard and Kaufman 1995), claims to authority were based on the twin themes of preserving national security in the face of the North Korean threat and centralizing power so as to marshall resources effectively in the drive toward industrialization and modernization.

But this portrait of the Korean presidency is fast becoming a vestige of the past. With nascent economic and social liberalization in Korea brought about by popular movements, the changing agendas of entrenched capital interests, and political reforms, the role of the presidency in Korea is undergoing fundamental change. The most striking outcome of this transformation will likely be a shift from a personality-centered presidential system to one which has an institutional form, in which presidents will have to share political power, be accountable to constitutional and legal expectations, be sensitive to the pressures of various societal and sectoral interests, and be resourceful in the use of bureaucratic counsel.

The transformation of the presidency from a strong authoritarian status to the product of a more democratized and decentralized system can be presented in heuristic terms. Figure 6.1 illustrates the transformation of the strong state to the weak state in comparison to Korea's developmental experience. Since the state has been dominated by the president, we can use presidential regimes as rough benchmarks to illustrate the transition. We have divided the Park regime into two periods, which roughly correspond to pre- and post-Yushin Constitution at the end of 1972. The Yushin Constitution was tantamount to an executive decree

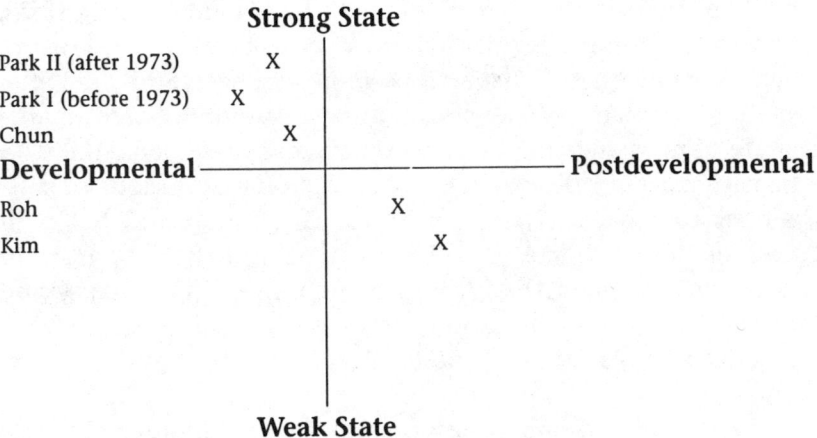

Figure 6.1: The Transformation of the Korean Presidency

by President Park which strengthened authoritarian power through the suspension of various civil liberties and other means. The figure illustrates that the Park and Chun regimes were characterized by strong state arrangements in the developmental context. As we have noted throughout the book, the breakdown of the developmental strong state arrangement occurred during the Chun regime. Both the Roh and Kim administrations reflect the weakening of state dominance over social and economic affairs as conditions start to reflect a postdevelopmental climate.

Korea's transformation presents both immediate and intermediate issues that require analysis and evaluation. In the short term, we should expect the president to act more as a broker among various, and often competing, interests in such areas as economic and social policy. Faced with the complexities of managing an advanced and diverse modern economy and addressing the need of increasingly aware and actualized individuals, we should also expect the president to come to rely on the advice and recommendations of bureaucratic actors. This is fundamentally different from an earlier era, when the president sought to impose his will on the direction of economic development and social policy priorities. Indeed, our research on technology development and transfer policy suggests this transformation is taking place.

In intermediate terms, the changes afoot in Korean society and economy suggest a number of potential developments in the presidency. First, in the face of maturing political institutions, such as the Korean legislature, court system, and local governments, presidents will have to be more responsive to the influence and demands of actors in these institutions. Second, the nature of party dynamics in Korea may change fundamentally. In the past, parties were essentially organizational extensions of presidential candidates. The fortunes of parties rose and fell with those of the candidate. It will be interesting to see if parties in Korea can free themselves from the moorings of personality and achieve a level of organization that will instead require potential candidates to bid for the support of party interests and membership.

To understand the transformation of developmental states into postdevelopmental states, we must understand how change affects the various institutions that make up the state. In the case of Korea, this requires an analysis of the presidency and the influence that change has had on this institution. We submit that the prospects of change will be fundamental. Where power once rested on authoritarian arrangements that placed a premium on the strength of personality and leadership, the basis of legitimacy for Korean presidents will turn on expectations associated with democratized societies. Public responsibility will increasingly be judged on terms set by major societal and sectoral actors, be they organized as parties, interest groups, or individuals. The test of presidential success will increasingly focus not on blunt claims of increasing gross domestic product or industrial capacity, but on the more subtle and complex dimensions of guiding the development of social and economic policy, understanding the role of the state in markets and society, mediating conflict among competing interests, and crafting effective coalitions to achieve policy success in an increasingly democratized society.

One of the most important institutional developments in postdevelopmental Korea involves the transformation of the bureaucracy. This transformation can be viewed from any number of perspectives, but two are particularly illustrative. First, the growing complexity of governance in a postdevelopmental era marked by pressing, and often cross-cutting, social and economic demands, combined with the uncertainties of global competition and technological complexity, changes the knowledge and hence the power differential between the president and the bureaucracy.

As we have noted throughout this book, the bureaucracy has been the one political institution which has been able to exercise some influence over the presidency over time. We argue that this influence is felt in both the advisory and implementation functions of the bureaucracy. Given the growing complexity of contemporary policy issues, the influence of the bureaucracy will necessarily increase. This will hold particularly true for matters dealing with technology policy.

Second, from a principal–agent perspective, the calculus of bureaucratic action and behavior will change profoundly. Under the strong president system, the principal–agent relationship was strongly in favor of the chief executive. Presidents Park and Chun, in particular, exercised dominating power over the bureaucracy. During the Roh and Kim administrations this power eased into a situation where bureaucratic actors exercised more influence in shaping policy. With the advent of term limits, the strengthening of the legislature, and the influence of the courts, the principal–agent relationship has been fundamentally altered. The resulting system of multiple principals seeks to influence a bureaucratic structure which enjoys growing influence over policy matters. This situation is further complicated by the role that organized interests, long controlled or suppressed by the state, may play in influencing and lobbying bureaucratic actors and agencies. In sum, the character of the bureaucracy in postdevelopmental Korea will be one of multiple principals, conflicting missions and objectives, and enhanced influence in matters relating to complex policy issues which require information gathering and expertise.

In order to deal with the demands and challenges of postdevelopmental society and the realities and expectations of postauthoritarian governance, the institution of the presidency is likely to grow and become more complex. We might well expect the office of the president to experience the growth in staff size and functions that we have seen in the American presidency. The growth of the institutional presidency in the United States has served to provide the information bases necessary to devise and carry out policy initiatives (see Pfiffner 1994; Kernell 1991; Burke 1992). As Dodd and Schott (1979) pointed out, the strengthening of the American presidency has been, in part, an effort to create a counterbalance to the growing influence of the bureaucracy. The growth of the institutional presidency in the United States has not resulted in an enhanced ability to impose prerogatives or will on other political actors and institutions. Instead, this growth has been seen as requisite to more effectively dealing with the demands of entrenched interests, other levels of governments, and other branches of government at the federal level.

As we have sought to describe, there have long been important distinctions between the Korean presidency and bureaucracy. Indeed, as we have stressed, failure to recognize differences in these two institutions provides an incomplete picture of the Korean experience. In the past, the president's absolute control meant that the bureaucracy followed the chief executive's lead in carrying out policy. Nonetheless, the bureaucracy held influence in policy formulation and implementation because of the practical demands of dealing with complex policy issues. Increasingly, we can expect that the bureaucracy's agenda may be at odds with the president's, especially as bureaucratic agents face pressures and demands from a variety of principals. In such situations, we may expect to see the president rely increasingly on his own personal bureaucracy made up of specialists and advisors in the Blue House. However, as noted in the American case by Pfiffner (1994), the drawback to such arrangements is that the rapid turnover of executive office staff leads to a lack of institutional memory. This becomes a disadvantage when compared to the deep institutional memory of bureaucratic agencies.

The Korean presidency faces institutional and legitimacy challenges that are familiar to the American system, but whose dimensions and degree are unique. As Pfiffner (1994) observed, cultural expectation and historic evolution have made the American presidency a distinctive institution which relies upon both symbolic and statutory power to achieve its ends. Under these arrangements, the societal nexus of the presidency is crucial because of the high degree of expectation placed upon the president to provide leadership and accountability. Similar circumstances exist in Korea, but are manifested in distinct ways. In Korea, the president has long been held to be the *personification* of the state. This is a product of both deep cultural roots and recent history. Korea's culture is anchored by the twin themes of Confucianism and authoritarianism (for discussions, see Jacobs 1985; Koo 1993b). This places a high degree of emphasis on hierarchy and deference to authority. The contours of recent history both reflect and serve to amplify this cultural orientation. As we have seen, until recently countervailing institutions, with the qualified exception of the bureaucracy, have been stunted in their development.

Given such a tradition, we should expect the Korean people to have high expectations for the efficacy of the president, even as the ability of the state to control social and economic conditions declines in the postdevelopmental state. It may be difficult to reconcile such beliefs in the face of conditions which will require the president to work more as a broker among contending interests and where technological, social, and economic events and circumstances will frequently point out the limits of the state. The Korean people, who have long seen the president as ultimately accountable for actions, have a tendency to be disappointed with the presidency. Indeed, this is part of the social fabric and, as a form of release, this is a none too surprising by-product of authoritarian culture. How such criticism will be manifested now that both the legislature and the press have greater freedom of expression is well worth considering. In order for Korea to democratize successfully, it may be necessary for the public to understand the limitations of the president. For Korea the danger remains that, in this fragile period of transformation and reform, the public's expectations of the president may be set too high. Such conditions could lead to a sense of antipathy and cynicism. Most troubling, such a climate could help to provide an opportunity for the return to authoritarian arrangements.

THE FUTURE OF THE POSTDEVELOPMENTAL STATE

In this book we have sought to examine and describe the structural and political factors that have contributed to Korea's developmental transition and the prospects of postdevelopmental conditions. We have restricted most of our discussion to recent and present circumstances. But our explorations lead us to offer briefly some observations about what the future might hold. While not wanting to be pessimistic, it is important to identify some of the potential dangers and circumstances that may be encountered in the postdevelopmental state. These, at least, include: (1) a tendency for the state to overcompensate in the face of declining influence, (2) the inability of nascent political institutions to respond to societal and economic demands for policy redress and action, (3) the deterioration of state sovereignty in the face of global economic and policy arrangements, and (4) the prospects of retrenchment by authoritarian factions.

The temptation to overcompensate in policy actions, especially as they relate to social and economic policy matters, is now part and parcel of the postmaterial and postindustrial experience. The logic of such action holds that as socioeconomic problems and conditions become more complex, often due to the influence of conditions exogenous to the borders or domain of the state, there will be the expectation that the state bears the responsibility for addressing the issue at hand. The litany of perceived policy failures which has come to dominate both political rhetoric and scholarly discourse bears evidence to the difficulties of governing and meeting public expectations in today's world. Indeed, such explanations of increased expectation and stressed capacities have been used to explain the implosion of complex institutional arrangements in industrialized Western democracies (see, particularly, Olson 1982; Lowi 1979; 1995). In a complex society marked by global markets, technological competition, and diverse social concerns, the limits of the state are being tested. The same holds true for the postdevelopmental state.

Postindustrial societies at least have the benefit of mature political institutions to handle the clamor and demand for policy action and behavior. Indeed, the resilience of the American political system is rooted in its many venues of access and articulation both across and among levels of government. An adjunct to this, of course, has been the presence of parties and interest groups that served to modulate discordant voices, present solutions to problems, and provide a vehicle for the expression of a range of interests. While much has been written about the dangers of hyperpluralism and the like (see Lowi 1979, for example), such a condition is probably far preferable to one in which divergent social forces are set loose without institutional arrangements to contain and guide them. For postdevelopmental states, such as Korea, which stand on the threshold of social and economic liberalization, the ability of both government and political institutions to be responsive to increased demands and responsibilities is uncertain.

The role of culture and shifting societal norms and values over time has been an important dimension of understanding the state experience through research carried out by Inglehart (1977) and others (see Abramson and Inglehart 1995; Granato, Inglehart, and Leblang 1996). Until recently, most of this research has focused on the experiences of industrialized democracies and the emergence of postmaterial value priorities that emphasize quality of life issues, as compared to material values that emphasize securing basic economic necessities of life (see, particularly, Inglehart 1977; 1990). More recently, the prospects of postmaterial sentiments in rapidly industrializing countries has been tentatively investigated. Research by Abramson and Inglehart (1995) suggest the presence of postmaterialist values in rapidly developing countries, such as Korea. The emergence of these values is nascent but indicative of a split between materialist and postmaterialist perspectives. This split is centered along generational lines, with postmaterialist values being most prominent among Korea's young adults (Abramson and Inglehart 1995:132–33). Though preferring to make distinctions along the lines of authoritarian and libertarian values, Aie-Rie Lee (1994:41) clearly describes this when noting that, "In the case of Korea, for instance, young people have been socialized to articulate their demands and interests through the Western-oriented education system and mass media. However, the political process has maintained, to a great extent, non-democratic modes of government." Such arrangements, as Lee notes, lead to a lack of congruence between popular expectations and institutional structures. This is manifested in the high level of cynicism found among Koreans toward policy institutions (Lee 1994:60). Because of this, the prospects for tolerance, trust, and patience toward these same institutions, which are at the center of political reform, are cast in doubt.

For Inglehart and his coauthors, postmaterial values are seen as supportive of democratic institutions and the product of relative economic prosperity. But in the absence of democratic institutions, such sentiments can be the source of discontent and activism that may disrupt existing institutional arrangements. As recent student demonstrations, labor strife, and other events in Korea illustrate, those pressing for postmaterial objectives may choose extrainstitutional routes of expression and action. The challenge of the postdevelopmental state is that its institutions may not be able to respond to these demands. Such circumstances may make it difficult for institutional arrangements to smoothly evolve into more democratic and participatory forms. Ideally, there will be postmaterialist institutions to handle postmaterialist needs, but this may not be the case in the postdevelopmental state.

The decline in the status of governmental institutions and dissatisfaction in the domestic sphere may be linked to the state's interaction with the international environment. The idea that nation-building requires independence from foreign intrusion and involvement is deeply rooted in history and has been embraced in the developmental experiences of some states. Thus, as we have seen, Korea sought to exclude foreign capital dominance through technology-transfer policy controls, especially licensing arrangements. Yet the contemporary nature of high-technology trade presents obstacles to successful implementation of licensing arrangements. Afraid to divulge trade secrets, foreign firms are more likely to demand direct-investment arrangements. Further reinforcing this trend is the fact that Korean firms have an interest in establishing direct-investment arrangements overseas. Added to this is the fact that the free flow of capital across boundaries is now generally seen as crucial to an efficient global economy. The prominence of neoclassical economic philosophies, which have informed various trade arrangements and international organizations, holds that foreign investment should be unfettered by the host state. The upshot of these conditions and factors is that the state is constrained from employing policy devices that might control the shape of foreign investment and international market interaction.

Economic activity leads to the organization of institutional arrangements that are intended to diminish the uncertainties of market activity. In this way, the rules of economic intercourse can be established, maintained, and enforced (see Ostrom 1991). In recent years, observers representing a variety of theoretical approaches have noted how the resulting institutions, which comprise the state, act not only to serve external economic interests but to perpetuate the interest of the state as well (for a review, see Geddes 1991). Nevertheless, as we have sought to demonstrate in the case of Korea, the interests of the state and major economic players are inextricably bound together. The social contract of the modern state and society in Korea might be framed in terms of mutually supportive arrangements between capital and institutional interests. While in the past, the state was the senior partner to capital interests, in recent years this relationship appears to have become reversed, with little intervening moments of parity between these partners. We are beginning to see how the needs of economic actors for market certainty may outstrip what the state is capable of providing. This leads to a crisis of legitimacy and utility for the state in terms of its ability to hold up its end of the bargain—minimizing market uncertainties. Declining ability to carry out this role through the provision of capital, the management of inflation and interest rates, subsidies for research, preferential regulations, and the like further marginalizes the state. This is a dilemma for all states, especially as we move to an era of global economy. But the contours of this dilemma are particularly defined for those postdevelopmental states, such as Korea, whose institutions have pinned so much of their fortunes on relationships with capital interests.

In a penetrating analysis of the resurgence of the state as foci of inquiry, Rockman (1990) identifies that the state can be conceptualized as taking three forms: (1) the decision-making state, which is able to command and bargain with major societal actors to accomplish policy ends; (2) the production aspects of the state, which are associated with the ability to provide and maintain desired resources and public goods for economic and social activity; and (3) the intermediary function of the state, where institutions provide the forum and function of resolving and addressing conflict and tensions among interests. The authoritarian era of the Korean modernization experience saw the state carrying out the first two of these functions with considerable influence and success. In the case of the decision-making role, the state, especially the president, enjoyed preeminence. This was secured because of the productional abilities of the state to control the extension of resources and public goods. The intermediary function of the state, however, was underdeveloped, limited as it was by interactions with capital interests and a studied strategy of ignoring and suppressing those voicing mass demands.

For postdevelopmental Korea, the ability of the state to function in the decision-making and production-oriented forms erodes. The transition to postdevelopmental status is abrupt. As Evans (1985) reminds us, the function of the state in regulating economic arrangements with external actors is paramount. But in the postdevelopmental era, such a role is diminished and cast in doubt. Evans (1985) argues that the role of the state in developmental stages is enhanced by transnational trade arrangements, because the state can play a critical gatekeeper role in coordinating trade and controlling local arrangements. But the postdevelopmental experience will likely contradict this assertion. A number of factors will converge to make this so, ranging from the declining ability of the Korean state to control domestic affairs due to the fragmentation of power across institutional lines and the devolution of responsibilities to local officials, to the growing independence of private-sector actors. Indeed, the emergence of Korean-based transnational companies, now engaged in direct-investment activities abroad, gives testimony to the increasing diversification and economic strength of Korean economic actors. Perhaps the postdevelopmental experience will parallel what Evans has outlined to be the case in advanced states. He observes that the role of the state is diminished in those states which become major capital exporters (Evans 1985:193).

The area where the Korean government has been most deficient, the intermediary function of the state, will be perhaps the most critical role for the postdevelopmental state. The credibility and legitimacy of Korea's policy-making and political institutions will rest on their ability to provide venues for deliberation and resolution, mediate conflict, and sustain constitutional stability. As we have emphasized, such demands require a reorientation for the role of the president, harbor significant changes for the bureaucracy, and will rely on responsiveness from those actors who heretofore have had a limited role in the Korean state, namely the legislature, courts, and local governments. It would be difficult enough to make these transitions if current economic and social conditions were held constant, but the complexities of international market factors, the contradicting demands of organized interests, and the passions of public opinion make the challenge even more acute.

The frustrations encountered in the postdevelopmental arena, be they dissatisfaction with quality of life issues, a sense of resentment for being on the losing end in international economic competition, or the loss of faith in new institutional arrangements, contribute to conditions which might allow for the resurgence of authoritarian power. We argue that this is the most dangerous possibility facing states that are undergoing regime transition. The nascent status of political and governmental institutions, the complexities of global market conditions, and other uncertainties of postdevelopmental societies make successful transformation a daunting enterprise. We hold that the ideal model of transformation is one that embraces democratic, participatory, and constitutionally based systems of governance.

As we have sought to stress throughout this book, the primary institutional actor in Korea will likely remain the president. Structural forces, such as tradition, culture, values, and history, as well as the obvious and rational self-interest of officeholders and allies in sustaining preeminence, suggests that the presidency will remain at the center of policy arrangements in Korea. But the characteristics of the postdevelopmental state will pose challenges for presidential leadership. Most simply put, the president may find himself in a vortex created by the cross-cutting demands of local and international priorities. Korea's entry onto the world economic stage is unprecedented and of historic dimension, but so too are reforms now taking place within Korea, where emphasis is being placed on devolving policy responsibilities to local governments. Matching citizen and community needs with the larger demands of international trade and competitiveness may prove difficult. Compounding this is the often-divisive nature of Korean regionalism, which has created rivalries across the country and flavored the nature of national politics (for discussions, see Han 1989; Han 1995; Choi 1993). The Kim administration has become sensitive to these cross-pressures and has emphasized the importance of "glocalization." Whether such a promise to mesh local and global priorities can be achieved remains to be seen. We can assert, however, that given the marginalization of the state in the face of social and economic change, the capacity of the state to influence outcomes will be diminished.

At the close of our century, regime transformation has become a distinguishing characteristic of many states. For good reason, much of our attention has been drawn to the transformations now under way in Eastern Europe and the former Soviet Union. But important transitions have been occurring elsewhere as well. A number of states which have recently gone through the developmental experience are also experiencing transformation. The experience of developmental state transition in Korea is particularly instructive, for here we are presented with a case in which a strong authoritarian market-oriented system is undergoing profound institutional and social change. As we have pointed out, Korea's authoritarian experience departed from the expected path, given the interpretations of developmental and modernization theories. Now the Korean experience, in moving away from authoritarianism, is providing new challenges for inquiry.

This book has explored the transition in the Korean state by focusing on the role of the presidency and the bureaucracy in charting the country's development objectives, policy strategies, and tactics. We have focused primarily on the changing role of the Korean presidency and its bureaucratic nexus in influencing state development. We note that there has been a twofold transition. First, broader social, historical, and economic effects are undermining the ability of the state (primarily the president and, to a lesser extent, the bureaucracy) to craft and successfully realize development policy goals. Second, the influence of the state vis-a-vis economic actors is in decline. We have sought to discuss these trends through an analytical framework that focuses on the dynamics of presidential–executive relationships.

While promising, the prospects for success in Korea are far from certain. The economic climate in Korea is highly influenced by international factors because of the economy's uncertain middle-ground status between highly developed economic powerhouses, such as Japan, and lower-wage developing states in East Asia. Capital interests in Korea should not necessarily be counted on to give allegiance to the nation's interests as they become transnational in character. Finally, Korea's lack of historical experience with democratic arrangements means that the foundations of participatory arrangements must be carefully cultivated.

NOTE

1. The relationship between presidents and constitutions is an interesting dimension of Korean politics. Under authoritarian arrangements, constitutions were essentially the codification of the ruling regime's aims. They served a symbolic function to legitimize rule. The current constitution, with its limits on presidential terms and focus on institutions and electoral procedures, marks a significant departure from the past. One of the most distinctive reasons for this is that the constitution was the product of agreements hammered out among contending parties in 1987, rather than the imposition of will by those in power (see Han 1989; Bedeski 1994).

References

Abramson, Paul R. and Ronald Inglehart. 1995. *Value Change in Global Perspective.* Ann Arbor: University of Michigan Press.

Ahn, Moonsuk. 1989. "Technology Innovation and Desirable Administrative System" (in Korean). Paper presented at the Symposium on Technology Innovation and Desirable Administrative System, Seoul.

———. 1995. "Administrative Reform in Kim Young-Sam's Government" (in Korean). *Proceedings of the International Seminar on Governmental Reform Policy.* Korean Association for Policy Studies, Seoul.

Allison, Graham. 1969. "Conceptual Models and the Cuban Missile Crisis." *American Political Science Review* 63(3):689–718.

Amsden, Alice. 1987. "Appropriate Technology," in *The New Palgrave Dictionary of Economics.* New York: W.W. Norton.

———. 1989. *Asia's Next Giant: South Korea and Late Industrialization.* New York: Oxford University Press.

Ashford, Douglas E. (ed.). 1992. *History and Context in Comparative Public Policy.* Pittsburgh: University of Pittsburgh Press.

Balassa, Bela. 1981. *The Newly Industrializing Countries in the World Economy.* New York: Pergamon.

Balassa, Bela (ed). 1982. *Development Strategies in Semi-Industrial Economies.* Baltimore: Johns Hopkins University Press.

Balassa, Bela. 1988. "The Interaction of Factor and Product Market Distortions in LDCs." *World Development* 16:449–464.

Bedeski, Robert. 1994. *The Transformation of South Korea: Reform and Reconstruction in the Sixth Republic Under Roh Tae Woo, 1987–1992.* London: Routledge.

Bell, Daniel. 1973. *The Coming Post-Industrial Society.* New York: Basic Books.

Bendor, Jonathan and Terry Moe. 1984. "An Adaptive Model of Bureaucratic Politics." *American Political Science Review* 79:755–774.

Bernard, Mitchell and John Ravenhill. 1995. "Beyond Product Cycles and Flying Geese: Regionalization, Hierarchy, and the Industrialization of East Asia." *World Politics* 47(1):171–209.

Branscomb, Lewis. 1991. "Toward a U.S. Technology Policy." *Issues in Science and Technology* (Summer):50–55.

Burke, John P. 1992. *The Institutional Presidency.* Baltimore: Johns Hopkins University Press.

Burkhart, Ross and Michael Lewis-Beck. 1994. "Comparative Democracy: The Economic Development Thesis." *American Political Science Review* 88(4):903–910.

Casper, Gretchen and Michelle Taylor. 1996. *Negotiating Democracy: Transitions from Authoritarian Rule.* Pittsburgh: University of Pittsburgh Press.

Chang, Ha Joon. 1993. "The Political Economy of Industrial Policy in Korea." *Cambridge Journal of Economics* 17:131–157.

Chenery, H. and A. Strout. 1966. "Foreign Assistance and Economic Development." *American Economic Review.* 56:679–733.

Cheng, Tun-Jen. 1990. "Political Regimes and Development Strategies: South Korea and Taiwan." Pp. 139–178 in Gary Gereffi and Donald Wyman (eds.). *Manufacturing Miracles.* Princeton: Princeton University Press.

Chilcote, Ronald. 1994. *Theories of Comparative Politics,* 2nd ed. Boulder, CO: Westview Press.

Chin, Hai-Sool. 1986. "Science and Technology Development Strategies: Experience of the Republic of Korea." Paper presented at the International Workshop on Formulation of Science and Technology Policy, Seoul.

Cho, Dong Sung. 1985. "Incentives and Restraints: Government Regulation of Direct Investment between Korea and the United States." In Karl Moskowitz (ed.). *From Patron to Partner.* Cambridge: Harvard University Press.

Choi, Hyungsup. 1986. *Technology Development in Developing Countries.* Tokyo: Asian Productivity Organization.

Choi, Jang Jip. 1993. "Political Cleavages in South Korea." Pp. 13–50 in Hagen Koo (ed.). *State and Society in Contemporary Korea.* Ithaca, NY: Cornell University Press.

Chou, Tein-Chen. 1988. "American and Japanese Direct Foreign Investment in Taiwan: A Comparative Study." *Hitotsubashi Journal of Economics* 29:165–177.

Chun, Sang Kun. 1982. *The Science and Technology Policy in Korea* (in Korean). Seoul: Jung-Ui Sa.

Chung, Chung-Kil. 1989. "Presidential Decisionmaking and Bureaucratic Expertise in Korea." *Governance* 2(3):267–292.

———. 1993. "A Desirable President's Policy Management for Economic Policy" (in Korean). *Korean Journal of Public Administration* 27:1–14.

Chung, Chung-Kil and Jong Sup Jun. 1991. "The Irony of Cutback Reform: The Korean Experience During a Period of Turbulent Transition." *International Review of Administrative Sciences* 57:45–57.

Clark, Cal and Steve Chan. 1994. "The Developmental Roles of the State: Moving Beyond the Developmental State in Conceptualizing Asian Political Economies." *Governance* 7(4):332–359.

———. 1995. "Do MNCs Matter for National Development?" Pp. 165–187 in S. Chan (ed.). *Foreign Direct Investment in a Changing World.* New York: St. Martin's.

Colclough, Christopher. 1991. "Structuralism versus Neo-liberalism: An Introduction." Pp. 1–25 in Christopher Colclough and James Manor (eds.). *States or Markets: Neo-Liberalism and the Development Policy Debate.* Oxford: Clarendon Press.

Collins, Susan. 1990. "Lessons from Korean Economic Growth." *American Economic Association Papers and Proceedings* 80(2):113–117.

Coolidge, Jefferson, Jr. 1981. "The Realities of Korean Foreign Investment Policy." *Asian Affairs* 12:370–385.

Cotton, James. 1992. "Understanding the State in South Korea: Bureaucratic-Authoritarian or State Economy Theory?" *Comparative Political Studies* 24(4):512–531.

Cumings, Bruce. 1987. "The Origins and Development of the Northeast Asian Political Economy: Industrial Sectors, Product Cycles, and Political Consequences." Pp. 44–83 in Frederic Deyo (ed.). *The Political Economy of the New Asian Industrialism.* Ithaca: Cornell University Press.

Deyo, F. C. (ed.). 1987. *The Political Economy of New Asian Industrialism.* Ithaca: Cornell University Press.

Dodd, Lawrence and Richard Schott. 1979. *Congress and the Administrative State.* New York: Wiley.

Donor, Richard. 1992. "Limits of State Strength: Toward an Institutionalist View of Economic Development." *World Politics* 44:398–431.

Douglas, Mary and Aaron Wildavsky. 1982. *Risk and Culture.* Berkeley: University of California Press.

Drysdale, Peter (ed.). 1972. *Direct Foreign Investment in Asia and the Pacific.* Toronto: University of Toronto Press.

Dunning, John. 1988. *Explaining International Production.* Boston: Unwin Hyman.

Ernst, Dieter. 1994. "What are the Limits to the Korean Model? The Korean Electronics Industry Under Pressure." Manuscript, Berkeley Roundtable on the International Economy.

Evans, David. 1991. "Visible and Invisible Hands in Trade Policy Reform." Pp. 26–47 in Christopher Colclough and James Manor (eds.). *States or Markets: Neo-Liberalism and the Development Policy Debate.* New York: Oxford University Press.

Evans, Peter. 1979. *Dependent Development: The Alliance of Multinational, State, and Local Capital in Brazil.* Princeton: Princeton University Press.

———. 1985. "Transnational Linkages and the Economic Role of the State: An Analysis of Developing and Industrializing Nations in the Post-World War II Period." Pp. 192–226 in Peter Evans, Dietrich Rueschemeyer, and Theda Skocpol (eds.). *Bring the State Back In.* Cambridge: Cambridge University Press.

———. 1987. "Class, State, and Dependence in East Asia: Lessons for Latin Americanists." Pp. 203–226 in Frederic Deyo (ed.). *The Political Economy of the New Asian Industrialism*. Ithaca: Cornell University Press.

———. 1995. *Embedded Autonomy: States and Industrial Transformation*. Princeton: Princeton University Press.

Evans, Peter, Dietrich Rueschemeyer, and Theda Skocpol. 1985. *Bringing the State Back In*. Cambridge: Cambridge University Press.

Fallows, James. 1994. *Looking at the Sun: The Rise of the New East Asian Economic and Political System*. New York: Vintage.

Ferrantino, Michael. 1992. "Technology Expenditures, Factor Intensity, and Efficiency in Indian Manufacturing." *Review of Economics and Statistics* 74:689–700

Fields, Karl. 1995. *Enterprise and the State in Korea and Taiwan*. Ithaca: Cornell University Press.

Frederickson, George. 1995. "Principles of Korean Public Administration in the Post-Development Decades: An American Perspective." Paper presented at the Conference on Korean Public Administration in the Post-Development Decades, Korea Institute of Public Administration, Seoul.

Furniss, Norman. 1992. "Functionalism and Policy Studies." Pp. 189–290 in Douglas Ashford (ed.). *History and Context in Comparative Public Policy*. Pittsburgh: University of Pittsburgh Press.

Gasiorowski, Mark. 1995. "Economic Crisis and Political Regime Change: An Event History Analysis." *American Political Science Review* 89(4): 882–897.

Geddes, Barbara. 1991. "Paradigms and Sand Castles in Comparative Politics of Developing Areas." Pp. 45–75 in William Crotty (ed.). *Political Science: Looking to the Future, Volume Two: Comparative Politics, Policy, and International Relations*. Chicago: Northwestern University Press.

Gilpin, Robert. 1975. *U.S. Power and the Multinational Corporation*. New York: Basic Books.

Glain, Steve. 1995. "Foreign Investment in South Korea Grew in 1994, but Others in Asia Fared Better." *Wall Street Journal* (January 13):A10.

Graham, Otis. 1992. *Losing Time: The Industrial Policy Debate*. Cambridge, MA: Harvard University Press.

Granato, Jim, Ronald Inglehart, and David Leblang. 1996. "The Effect of Cultural Values on Economic Development: Theory, Hypotheses, and Some Empirical Tests." *American Journal of Political Science* 40(3):607–631.

Griffin, K. and J. Enos. 1970. "Foreign Assistance: Objectives and Consequences." *Economic Development and Cultural Change* :313–327.

Haggard, Stephan. 1990. *Pathways from the Periphery: The Politics of Growth in the Newly Industrializing Countries*. Ithaca: Cornell University Press.

Haggard, Stephan and Robert Kaufman. 1995. *The Political Economy of Democratic Transitions*. Princeton: Princeton University Press.

Haggard, Stephan and Sylvia Maxfield. 1996. "The Political Economy of Financial Internationalization in the Developing World." *International Organization* 50(1):35–68.

Haggard, Stephan and Chung-in Moon. 1990. "Institutions and Economic Policy: Theory and a Korean Case Study." *World Politics* 42:210–237.

Hahm, Sung Deuk. 1994. "Political and Administrative Arrangements for Technology Innovation in Korea." *Korean Policy Studies Review* 4(2):54–73.

Hahm, Sung Deuk and L. Christopher Plein. 1995. "Institutions and Technological Development In Korea: The Role of the President." *Comparative Politics* 28:55–76.

Hahm, Sung Deuk, L. Christopher Plein, and Richard Florida. 1994. "The Politics of International Technology Transfer: Lessons from the Korean Experience." *Policy Studies Journal* 22(2):311–321.

Hall, Peter. 1986. *Governing the Economy: The Politics of State Intervention in Britain and France*. New York: Oxford University Press.

Han, Sang-Jin. 1995. "Media and Mediations: The Public Sphere in Korea's Democratic Transition." Paper presented at the Georgetown Conference on Korean Society, Washington, DC.

Han, Sung-Joo. 1989. "South Korea: Politics in Transition." Pp. 266–303 in Larry Diamond, Juan Line, and Seymour Martin Lipset (eds.). *Democracy in Developing Countries: Asia*, Volume 3. Boulder, CO: Lynn Reinner, Publishers.

Hanbek Delphi Research Team. 1995. "Changing Role of Bureaucracy." *Forum 21* (Spring):54–61.

Hankuk Ilbo. 1993. (December 17):12.

Harsanyi, John. 1969. "Rational-Choice Models of Political Behavior vs. Functionalist and Conformist Theories." *World Politics* 21(4):513–538.

Hart, Jeffrey. 1992. "The Effects of State-Societal Arrangements on International Competitiveness: Steel, Motor Vehicles and Semiconductors in the United States, Japan, and Western Europe." *British Journal of Political Science* 22:225–300.

Helleiner, Gerald. 1989. "Transnational Corporation and Direct Foreign Investment." Pp. 1469–1474 in *Handbook of Development Economics*, Vol. 2. Amsterdam: North-Holland.

Hofferbert, Richard. 1974. *The Study of Public Policy*. Indianapolis: Bobbs-Merrill.

Hufbauer, G. C. 1970. "The Impact of National Characteristics and Technology on the Commodity Composition of Trade in Manufactured Goods." Pp. 145–231 in R. Vernon (ed.). *The Technology Factor in International Trade*. New York: Columbia University Press.

Hyun, Won Bok. 1986. *An Analytical Study of the Science and Technology Policy During the Early Part of 1980's* (in Korean). Seoul: Korea Science and Engineering Foundation.

Im, Hyug Baeg. 1990. "The Rise of Bureaucratic Authoritarianism in South Korea." *World Politics* 42:231–257.

————. 1995. "Between the Market and the State: Prospects for an Associative Model of Industrial Relations in Korea." Paper presented at the Georgetown Conference on Korean Society, Washington, DC.

Inglehart, Ronald. 1977. *The Silent Revolution.* Princeton: Princeton University Press.

————. 1990. *Culture Shift in Advanced Industrial Society.* Princeton: Princeton University Press.

Jacobs, Norman. 1985. *The Korean Road to Modernization and Development.* Urbana, IL: University of Illinois Press.

Johnson, Chalmers. 1982. *MITI and the Japanese Miracle: The Growth of Industrial Policy, 1925–1975.* Stanford: Stanford University Press.

————. 1987. "Political Institutions and Economic Performance: The Government-Business Relationship in Japan, South Korea, and Taiwan." Pp. 136–164 in Frederic Deyo (ed.). *The Political Economy of the New Asian Industrialism.* Ithaca: Cornell University Press.

Jones, Leary and Il Sakong. 1980. *Government, Business, and Entrepreneurship in Economic Development: The Korean Case.* Cambridge: Harvard University Press.

Jun, Jong S. and Jae Poong Yoon. 1995. "Korean Public Administration at a Crossroads: Culture, Development, and Change." In Ahmed Shafigul Huque, et al., *Public Administration in the Newly Industrialized Countries.* New York: Macmillan.

Jung, Yong-duck. 1995. "Governmental Reorganizations in Korea" (in Korean). *Korean Policy Studies Review* 4(1):58–84.

Justman, Moshe and Morris Tuebal. 1988. "A Framework for an Explicit Industry and Technology Policy for Israel and Some Specific Proposals." In C. Freeman and B. Lundvall (eds.). *Small Countries Facing the Technological Revolution.* London: Pinter Publishers.

Kang, David. 1995. "South Korea and Taiwanese Development and the New Institutional Economics." *International Organization* 49(3):555–587.

Kang, Mun Gu. 1995. "Democratic Transition at Crossroads: Abnormalities in State-Society Relationship in South Korea." Paper presented at the annual meeting of the American Political Science Association, Chicago.

Kasza, Gregory. 1987. "Bureaucratic Politics in Radical Military Regimes." *American Political Science Review* 81(3):851–872.

Kennedy, William. 1987. *Industrial Structure: Capital Markets and the Origins of British Economic Decline.* Cambridge: Cambridge University Press.

Kernell, Samuel. 1991. "The Evolution of the White House Staff." Pp. 43–60 in James Pfiffner (ed). *The Managerial Presidency.* Pacific Grove, CA: Brooks/Cole Publishing.

Kim, Eun Mee. 1992. "The Investments of U.S. and Japanese Multinational Corporations in Korea: A Comparative Investigation." *Asian Affairs* 18(4):214–227.

————. 1993. "Contradictions and Limits of a Developmental State: With Illustrations from the South Korean Case." *Social Problems* 40(2):228–249.

————. 1994. "Socioeconomic Development in South Korea." *In Depth* (Spring):3–39.

Kim, Eui-Young. 1993. "The Developmental State and the Politics of Business Interest Associations: The Case of the Textile Industry in South Korea." *Pacific Focus* 8:31–60.

Kim, Linsu and Karl Dahlman. 1992. "Technology Policy for Industrialization: The Integrative Framework and Korea's Experience." *Research Policy* 21:437–452.

Kim, Pan S. 1993. "Public Bureaucracy and Regionalism in South Korea." *Administration and Society* 25(August).

Kim, Taekwon. 1994. "Technological Complexity and Technology Policy: With Application to the Case of South Korea." *Pacific Focus* 9:95–124.

Kim, Young-Woo. 1986. "Policy for Promoting Science and Technology in Korea." Paper presented at the International Workshop on Formulation of Science and Technology Policy, Seoul.

Kim, Young Sam. 1994. "Reforming While Forging Ahead." *Presidents & Prime Minister.* (March/April):4–6.

Kim, Yong Cheol. 1994. "Administrative Neutralism and the Politics of Survival: Labor Policy Under Park Chung Hee, 1961–1971." *Pacific Focus* 9:125–152.

Kim, Kwang Woong. 1991. *Study of Korean Bureaucracy* (in Korean). Seoul: Daeyoung Moonhwasa.

Kitschelt, Herbert. 1992. "Political Regime Change: Structure and Process-Driven Explanations?" *American Political Science Review* 86(4):1028–1034

Kohno, Masaru. 1992. "Rational Foundations for the Organization of the Liberal Democratic Party in Japan." *World Politics* 44:369–397

Kojima, Kiyoshi. 1973. "A Macroeconomic Approach to Foreign Direct Investment." *Hitotsubashi Journal of Economics* 14:1–14.

————. 1977. "Transfer of Technology to Developing Countries-Japanese Types versus American Type." *Hitotsubashi Journal of Economics* 18:1–14.

————. 1978. *Direct Foreign Investment: A Japanese Model of Multinational Business Operations.* New York: Praeger.

————. 1985. "Japanese and American Direct Investment in Asia: A Comparative Analysis." *Hitotsubashi Journal of Economics* 26:1–35.

Koo, Hagen. 1987. "The Interplay of State, Social Class, and World System in East Asian Development: The Cases of South Korea and Taiwan." Pp. 165–181 in Frederic Deyo (ed.). *The Political Economy of the New Asian Industrialism.* Ithaca: Cornell University Press.

————. 1990. "From Farm to Factory: Proletarianization in Korea." *American Sociological Review* 55:669–681.

———. 1991. "Middle Class, Democratization and Class Formation: The Case of South Korea." *Theory and Society* (Summer).

———. 1993a. *The State and Society in Contemporary Korea.* Ithaca, NY: Cornell University Press.

———. 1993b. "Strong State and Contentious Society." Pp. 231–249 in Hagen Koo (ed). *The State and Society in Contemporary Korea.* Ithaca, NY: Cornell University Press.

Korea Advanced Institute of Science and Technology. 1986. *A Study on Science and Technology Development System in Korea and its Future Direction.* Seoul: Korean Advanced Institute of Science and Technology.

Korean Economic Planning Board. 1985. *Major Statistics of the Korean Economy,* Seoul: Korean Economic Planning Board.

Korean Ministry of Commerce and Industry. 1986. *Plan for the Strengthening of Industrial Competitive Power* (in Korean). Seoul: Korean Ministry of Commerce and Industry.

Korean Ministry of Science and Technology. 1980. "The Plan for Consolidation and Operation of Research and Development System" (in Korean). Seoul: Korean Ministry of Science and Technology.

———. 1981. "The Fifth Five-Year Science and Technology Development Plan, 1982–1986" (in Korean). Seoul: Korean Ministry of Science and Technology.

———. 1982. "Improvement Plan on Government Direct Funding System on Research and Development" (in Korean). Seoul: Korean Ministry of Science and Technology.

———. 1985. "Plan for Efficient Operation of Government Supported Research Institutes" (in Korean). Seoul: Korean Ministry of Science and Technology.

———. 1986a. "Plan for the Improvement and Efficient Operation of Science and Technology Administrative System" (in Korean). Seoul: Korean Ministry of Science and Technology.

———. 1986b. *Science and Technology Annual.* Seoul: Korean Ministry of Science and Technology.

———. 1987. "White Paper on National Research and Development Project" (in Korean). Seoul: Korean Ministry of Science and Technology.

———. 1993. *Introduction to Science and Technology Republic of Korea.* Seoul: Korean Ministry of Science and Technology.

Krueger, Anne. 1979. *The Developmental Role of the Foreign Sector and Aid.* Cambridge: Harvard University Press.

———. 1990. "Asian Trade and Growth Lessons." *American Economic Association Papers and Proceedings* 80(2):108–112.

———. 1995. *Trade Policies and Developing Nations.* Washington D.C.: The Brookings Institution.

Kuo, Cheng-Tian. 1994. "Private Governance in Taiwan." Paper presented at the annual meeting of the Midwest Political Science Association. Chicago.

Lall, Sangyat. 1993. "Understanding Technology Development," *Development and Change* 24:719–753.

Lee, Aie-Rie. 1994. "Culture Shift and Politicalization in the Korean Mass Public." *In Depth* 4(2):41–64.

Lee, Chung. 1980. "United States and Japanese Direct Investment in Korea: A Comparative Study." *Hitotsubashi Journal of Economics* 20:26–41.

———. 1984. "Transfer of Technology From Japan and the United States to Korean Manufacturing Industries: A Comparative Study." *Hitotsubashi Journal of Economics* 25:125–136.

Lee, Hahn Been. 1993. "Korean Economic Development Revisited." Paper presented at the Plekhanov Russian Economic Academy, Moscow.

Lipset, Seymour. 1959. "Some Social Requisites of Democracy." *American Political Science Review* 53:69–105

Lowi, Theodore. 1979. *The End of Liberalism: Ideology, Policy, and the Crisis of Public Authority.* New York: Wiley.

———. 1995. *The End of the Republican Era.* Norman, OK: University of Oklahoma Press.

Manor, James. 1991. "Politics and Neo-Liberals." Pp. 279–305 in Christopher Colclough and James Manor (eds.). *States or Markets: Neo-Liberalism and the Development Policy Debate.* New York: Oxford University Press.

Mardon, Russell. 1990. "The State and the Effective Control of Foreign Capital: The Case of South Korea." *World Politics* 43(1):111–138.

Mardon, Russell and W.K. Paik. 1992. "The State, Foreign Investment, and Sustaining Industrial Growth in South Korea and Thailand." In C. Clark and S. Chan (eds.), *The Evolving Pacific Basin in the Global Political Economy: Domestic and International Linkage.* Boulder: Lynne Reinner.

Mason, R. 1980. "A Comment on Professor Kojima's Japanese Type versus American Type of Technology Transfer." *Hitotsubashi Journal of Economics* 20(2):48–50.

Mitchell, Timothy. 1991. "The Limits of the State: Beyond Statist Approaches and Their Critics." *American Political Science Review* 85(1):77–96.

Monroe, Kristen Renwick. 1991. "The Theory of Rational Action: What is it? How Useful is it for Political Science?" Pp. In 77–98 in William Crotty (ed). *Political Science: Looking to the Future, Volume One: The Theory and Practice of Political Science.* Chicago: Northwestern University Press.

Moon, Chung-in. 1990. "Beyond Statism: The Political Economy of Growth in South Korea." *International Studies Notes* 15(1):24–27.

Moon, Chung-in and Rashemi Prasad. 1994. "Beyond the Developmental State: Institutions, Networks, and Politics." *Governance* 7(4):360–386.

Nordlinger, Eric. 1981. *On the Autonomy of the Democratic State.* Cambridge: Harvard University Press.

O'Donnell, Guillermo. 1973. *Modernization and Bureaucratic Authoritarianism: Studies in Latin American Politics.* Berkeley, CA: University of California Press.

Oh, John Kie-chiang. 1994. "Anti-Americanism and Anti-Authoritarian Politics in Korea." *In Depth* Spring:65–82.

Okimoto, Daniel. 1989. *Between MITI and the Market: Japanese Industrial Policy for High Technology.* Stanford: Stanford University Press.

Olson, Mancur. 1982. *The Rise and Decline of Nations: Economic Growth, Stagflation, and Social Rigidities.* New Haven: Yale University Press.

Ostrom, Elinor. 1991. "Rational Choice Theory and Institutional Analysis: Toward Complementarity." *American Political Science Review* 85(1):237–243.

Ostry, Sylvia and Richard R. Nelson. 1995. *Techno-Nationalism and Techno-Globalism: Conflict and Cooperation.* Washington, D.C.: The Brookings Institution.

Ozawa, Terutomo. 1979. *Multinationalism, Japanese Style.* Princeton: Princeton University Press.

Pack, Howard and Larry E. Westphal. 1986. "Industrial Strategy and Technological Change." *Journal of Development Economics* 22:87–128.

Papanek, G. 1973. "Aid Foreign Private Investment, Savings and Growth in Less Developed Countries." *Journal of Political Economy* 81:120–130.

Park, Chong-Min. 1991. "Authoritarian Rule in South Korea." *Asian Survey.* 21(8): 743–761.

Pfiffner, James. 1994. *The Modern Presidency.* New York: St. Martin's Press.

Pollard, Sidney. 1985. "Capital Exports, 1870–1914: Harmful or Beneficial?" *Economic History Review* 38:489–514.

Presidential Council on Science and Technology. 1991. "Policy Recommendations of the Presidential Council on Science and Technology for the President" (in Korean). Seoul.

———. 1993. "Role and Organization of the Presidential Council on Science and Technology" (in Korean). Seoul.

Ranis, G. and Fei, J. 1975. "A Model of Growth and Employment in the Open Dualistic Economy: The Cases of Korea and Taiwan." In F. Stewart (ed.). *Employment, Income Distribution and Development.* London: Frank Cass.

Rockman, Bert A. 1990. "Minding the State—or A State of Mind?" *Comparative Political Studies.* 23(1):25–55.

Roemer, John. 1975. "U.S.-Japanese Competition in International Markets: A Study of the Trade-Investment Cycle in Modern Capitalism." Research Paper 22, Institute of International Studies, University of California at Berkeley.

———. 1976. "Japanese Direct Foreign Investment in Manufactures: Some Comparison with US Pattern." *Quarterly Review of Economics and Business* 16:98–107.

Rosenstein-Rodan, P. N. 1961. "International Aid for Underdeveloped Countries." *Review of Economics and Statistics* 43:391–408.

Schmidt, Vivien. 1996. *From State To Market? The Transformation of French Business and Government*. New York: Cambridge University Press.

Simon, Herbert. 1947. *Administrative Behavior*. New York: Free Press.

Skolnikoff, Eugene. 1993. *The Elusive Transformation: Science, Technology, and International Politics*. Princeton: Princeton University Press.

Steers, Richard, Yoo Shin, and Gerado Ungson. 1989. *The Chaebol: Korea's New Industrial Might*. New York: Harper & Row.

Stobaugh, Robert and Louis Wells. (eds). 1984. *Technology Crossing Borders*. Boston: Harvard Business School Press.

Toye, John. 1991. "Is There a New Political Economy of Development." Pp. 321–338 in Christopher Colclough and James Manor, (eds.). *States or Markets: Neo-Liberalism and the Development Policy Debate*. Oxford: Clarendon Press.

U.S. Department of Commerce. 1988. *International Direct Investment*. Washington D.C.: United States Government Printing Office.

Wade, Robert. 1990. *Governing the Market: Economic Theory and the Role of Government in East Asian Industrialization*. Princeton: Princeton University Press.

———. 1992. "East Asia's Economic Success: Conflicting Perspectives, Partial Insights, Shaky Evidence." *World Politics* 45(2):270–320.

Watanuki, Joji. 1995. "State and Civil Society in Contemporary East Asia: Beyond the Developmental State." Paper presented at the Georgetown Conference on Korean Society, Washington, DC.

Weisskopf, T. 1972. "The Impact of Foreign Capital Inflow on Domestic Savings in Underdeveloped Countries." *Journal of International Economics* 3:25–38.

Westphal, Larry. 1978. "The Republic of Korea's Experience with Export-Led Industrial Development." *World Development* 6:347–382.

———. 1990. "Industrial Policy in an Export-Propelled Economy: Lessons from South Korea's Experience." *Journal of Economic Perspective* 4(3): 41–59.

Westphal, Larry, Linsu Kim, and Carl, J. Dahlman. 1985. "Reflections on the Republic of Korea's Acquisition of Technological Capability." Pp. 167–221 in Rosenberg, Nathan and Frischtak, Claudio (ed.). *International Technology Transfer*, New York: Praeger Publishers.

White, G. 1988. *Developmental States in East Asia*. London: Macmillan.

Wilson, Graham. 1995. "Rationality, Bureaucrats, and Politicians in Westminster Model Systems." Paper presented at the Structure and Organization of Government Conference, Seoul.

Woo, Jung-En. 1991. *Race to Swift*. New York: Columbia University Press.

World Bank. 1993. *The East Asian Miracle: Economic Growth and Public Policy*. New York: Oxford University Press.

Yang, Yoonsae. 1972. "Foreign Investments in Developing Countries: Korea." Pp. 242–257 in Peter Drysdale (ed.). *Direct Foreign Investment in Asia and the Pacific*. Toronto: University of Toronto Press.

Yeom, Jaeho. 1989. "A Bureaucratic Organization in Network Setting: MITI and Japanese Industrial Policy for High Technology." PhD Dissertation, Stanford University.

Yoo, Joon Sang. 1988. "The Role of Political Party and the Legislature in Science and Technology Development" (in Korean). Paper presented at the National Congress for the Advancement of Technology, Seoul.

Yoon, Young-Kwan. 1990. "The Political Economy of Transition: Japanese Foreign Direct Investments in the 1980s." *World Politics* 43:1–27.

Yu, Hee-Yol, 1986. "Technology Transfer Policy in Korea." Paper presented at the International Workshop on Formulation of Science and Technology Policy, Seoul.

Index

About the Authors

Sung Deuk Hahm received his Ph.D. in public policy analysis at Carnegie-Mellon University and is now director of the Advanced Program in Policy Studies of the Graduate School of Policy Studies and assistant professor of public policy at Korea University. He was director of the Georgetown Center for Asian Public Policy and assistant professor of public policy and business administration at Georgetown University. He was also managing editor of *Governance: An International Journal of Policy and Administration,* published by Basil Blackwell Press of Oxford. During the completion of his dissertation, he was assistant professor of public administration and political science at West Virginia University while working as a research associate at the Ronald Reagan Presidential Center for Public Affairs in Simi Valley, California, and the John F. Kennedy School of Government at Harvard University. He was also a visiting scholar at the Hoover Institution at Stanford University. His doctoral dissertation received an Honorable Mention for Outstanding Dissertation from the National Association of Schools for Public Affairs and Administration (NASPAA). He received the Raymond Vernon Prize for the best article in the 1992 *Journal of Policy Analysis and Management.* His research interests are in the areas of Korean presidency, international political economy, public budgeting & finance, and industrial policy. He has published over twenty-five articles in scholarly journals and edited books such as *Comparative Politics, Journal of Public Policy, Comparative Political Studies, American Politics Quarterly,* and *Public Administration Review.* Professionally, he was a program co-chair of the 1997 National Research Conference of the American Society for Public Administration (ASPA) and a member of the editorial board for the *Journal of Public Administration Research and Theory.* Also, he has been a consultant for Ernst & Young, LLP.

L. Christopher Plein is an assistant professor of public administration at West Virginia University. He received his Ph.D. in Political Science from the University of Missouri, Columbia. His research interests include science and technology policy, comparative policy and administration, and agenda setting research. His work, as author or coauthor, has been published in various books and in such journals as *Comparative Politics, Policy Studies Journal,* and *Science, Technology & Human Values.*